Walking the Coastline
of Shetland

No. 4

Northmavine

Walking the Coastline of Shetland

No. 4

Northmavine

Peter Guy

The coastline and circular walks in Northmavine
and the islands of Uyea and Gluss

The Shetland Times Ltd.,
Lerwick, Shetland.
2006

First published by The Shetland Times Ltd., 2006

ISBN 1 904746 17 9
ISBN 978 1 904746 17 1

A CIP catalogue record for this book is available from the British Library.

Books in the same series

No. 1 The Island of Yell
No. 2 The Island of Unst
No. 3 The Island of Fetlar
No. 5 Westside
No. 6 South Mainland
No. 7 Eastside

Dedicated to the memory of John Williamson ("Johnnie Notions")
James Inkster, Jack Rattar and Dr Tom Anderson, all Northmavine men
who contributed to and helped preserve the heritage of Shetland.

Cover Photographs:

Front cover – Lang Ayre © Bruce Wilcock
Inserts: Fethaland fishing station ruins © Peter Guy
Ronas Hill information cairn, Collafirth Hill © Peter Guy
Stacks of Stoura Pund, Brei Wick © Catherine Ginger

Back cover: The Drongs from Heads of Grocken © Catherine Ginger

Printed and published by
The Shetland Times Ltd., Gremista, Lerwick,
Shetland ZE1 0PX, Scotland.

"I love to walk where none had walk'd before,
About the rocks that ran along the shore;
Or far beyond the sight of men to stray,
And take my pleasure when I lost my way,
For then 'twas mine to trace the hilly heath.
And all the mossy moor that lies beneath.
Here had I favourite stations, where I stood
And heard the murmurs of the ocean flood,
With not a sound beside."

George Crabbe (1754 - 1832)

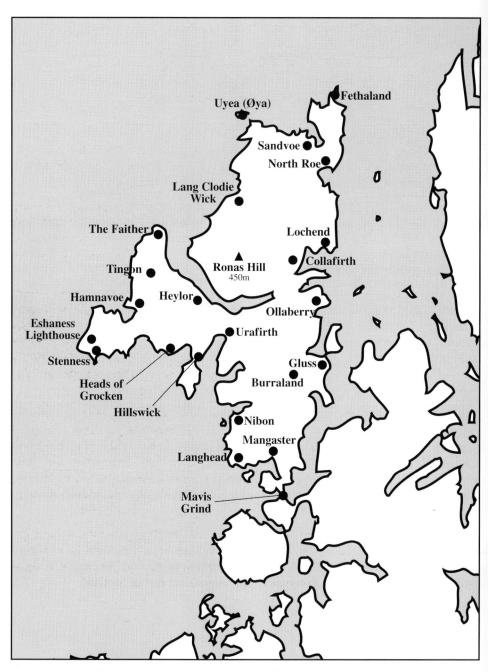

**Northmavine showing start and finishing points of the
Round Northmavine Trek and Circular Cross-Country Walks.**

Walking the Coastline of Shetland No. 4

NORTHMAVINE

(120 Miles / 200 Kilometres)

Northmavine, lying north of Mavis Grind, is the largest parish in Shetland. It is part of the island of Mainland, Shetland's largest island, but is almost an island itself as the neck of land connecting it to the mainland is only 100 yards or so across.

The area excels in wild rock scenery but there are also many parts of pleasant cultivated land and one can enjoy the tremendous contrast between the red colour of the cliffs with the green of the grazing land that surmounts them. There are also many scenic voes and lochs in the area which is seventeen miles at its longest from north to south and eleven miles at its broadest from east to west.

To the north the horizon is dominated by Shetland's highest hill, Ronas Hill (1,486ft, 450m) and the Northmavine Trek includes the peak of this hill on its route. It is pretty bleak up there and indeed on other parts of the west coast, so a walker needs to be properly equipped. Be prepared and carry too much rather than too little. The views are often spectacular all round the coastline but it is essential to remember Alfred Wainwright's dictum, "Watch your feet whilst walking – stop to enjoy a view". There are other walks to be enjoyed after Northmavine!

There have been many brilliant descriptions of the attractions to be seen in Northmavine by various travel writers over the years. Inevitably Hillswick and Eshaness get good coverage but these are but two small areas in a vast landscape. There is something of interest in every mile of the 120 miles round the coast. Walkers are generally welcomed everywhere, provided they do not damage fences or crops or frighten livestock by bringing dogs into grazing areas. If in doubt about any matter ask the advice from somebody in the local crofting community. Advice and information is usually cheerfully given.

The Northmavine Trek is divided into fourteen sections purely because that is the way I walked it. I have allowed a pace of two miles an hour but experienced long distance walkers will travel faster than that. There are also fifteen suggestions for circular walks so there should be something for everyone in this magnificent part of Shetland.

Good walking!

Peter Guy
Overby
Burravoe
Yell
2006

SAFETY AND CONSERVATION

Be Prepared

Have a knowledge of basic First Aid.

Know how to navigate properly using map and compass.

Carry the OS map (maps) appropriate to the walk being undertaken.

Select the right equipment for walking. Carry waterproofs, spare sweater, whistle, food, torch, gloves and balaclava.

Leave word of your planned walk and report your return.

Respect the land

Access: The Land Reform (Scotland) Act 2003 clearly sets down in statute a presumption in favour of access. The Act came into force in 2004 and the Scottish Outdoor Access Code has been approved by the Scottish Parliament and local authorities have begun to take up new powers. Walkers are reminded that this is an extremely sensitive issue in some parts of Scotland and we should remain mindful of the needs of those who work the land.

Take care not to drop litter. It is unsightly and can be dangerous to animals.

Remember to use gates or stiles where possible instead of climbing fences and walls.

Park with consideration, remembering that agricultural vehicles may need access near where you leave a car.

Keep dogs under full control. Remember, crofters are entitled to shoot dogs found worrying sheep.

Cliffs can present the greatest hazard and when geos (creeks) bite deep into the cliffs, the drop may be out of sight until the last moment. Keep "well in" and wear boots that give some traction on grassy slopes.

Be weatherwise

Exercise caution in low cloud or mist.

On cliffs windy and misty conditions can create dangerous situations.

Aim to complete a walk in daylight hours.

■ WALKING THE COASTLINE OF SHETLAND NO. 4 ■

NORTHMAVINE

120 Miles (200 Kilometres)

Section	From	To	Miles	Kms	Hrs	Page
1	MAVIS GRIND	MANGASTER	5	8	3	13
2	MANGASTER	NIBON	5	8	3	16
3	NIBON	URAFIRTH	9	15	5	19
4	URAFIRTH	HILLSWICK	8	13	4	23
5	HILLSWICK	STENNESS	9	15	4	26
6	STENNESS	HAMNAVOE	8	13	6	31
7	HAMNAVOE	HEYLOR	8	13	4	38
8	HEYLOR	NORTH COLLAFIRTH	6	10	3	42
9	NORTH COLLAFIRTH	LANG CLODIE WICK	10	17	5	45
10	LANG CLODIE WICK	SANDVOE	10	17	5	49
11	SANDVOE	NORTH ROE	12	20	6	53
12	NORTH ROE	OLLABERRY	13	23	6	59
13	OLLABERRY	GLUSS ISLE	8	13	4	63
14	GLUSS ISLE	MAVIS GRIND	9	15	4	66
		TOTAL	120	200	66	

CIRCULAR WALKS

Section	From	To	Miles	Kms	Hrs	Page
A	MANGASTER	LANG HEAD	6	10	3	69
B	NIBON		4	6	2	72
C	NESS OF HILLSWICK		4	8	3	75
D	STENNESS	ESHANESS LIGHTHOUSE	4	6	2	79
E	ESHANESS LIGHTHOUSE	HAMNAVOE	9	15	5	83
F	HAMNAVOE	TINGON	5	8	3	86
G	HEYLOR		6	10	3	88
H	COLLAFIRTH	RONAS HILL	6	10	3	90
I	COLLAFIRTH	LANG CLODIE WICK	15	20	7	93
J	NORTH ROE	UYEA ISLE	10	17	5	97
K	ISBISTER	FETHALAND	6	10	3	101
L	LOCHEND	GIANT'S TRAIL	5	8	3	105
M	OLLABERRY	QUEYFIRTH	5	8	3	110
N	GLUSS	BURRALAND	5	8	5	112
O	BREIWICK	GROCKEN	5	8	3	116

A NOTE ON SOME HISTORICAL ACCOUNTS OF NORTHMAVINE

Northmavine has some of the finest and most rugged scenery in Shetland. It also abounds in historical monuments and signs of ancient habitation by man are evident not only on the sheltered voes of the eastern coastline but even on top of Ronas Hill itself. There are many burial sites dating back to Neolithic and Early Bronze Age times, settlements, burnt mounds and standing stones. Eight brochs were possibly built here during the Iron Age 100 BC-AD 200, four of them remaining in some clear form today.

At some time in the 'Dark Ages' Celtic Christian Missionaries arrived to convert the Picts and a cliff settlement at the Kame of Isbister is thought to have been a monastic community. The area has, sadly, suffered from depopulation as a result of crofting 'clearances' in the 19th century and the decline in fishing. However, crofting and fishing still play an important part in the economic life of the Northmavine community. There have also been quarrying operations using the 'hollow tooth' method of extraction to minimise visual environmental impact at ground level. Sullom Voe Terminal, Europe's largest oil terminal, lies opposite the SE coast line of Northmavine and many people from the parish are employed there. The activity in Sullom Voe would certainly startle any of the previous visitors, who would never have imagined such a construction could have ever been conceived let alone established in such an area. We can barely believe it ourselves today!

John Brand (1701) thought, "this Country is generally Mossy, soft and spungey". He reported that, "behind the place where the altar stood at the Cross Kirk, Eshaness and beneath the pulpit were found several pieces of silver in various shapes brought by afflicted people, in the form of a head, arm or foot."

Thomas Gifford (1733), "It is the largest parish in Zetland but not the most populous. It is all mountains, covered with heath and marshes; a vast many lakes and burns abounding with trouts. On the east side of this parish is a small bay of the sea, running up forth about eight miles dividing betwixt the parishes of Delting and Northmaven, all good anchor ground, but very little frequented by ships." (He is referring to Sullom Voe!)

George Low (1774) regretted that the, "expense and the precariousness of the weather keep the fishermen always poor and for the most part indebted to their masters. In Northmaven much loss of men at sea."

Samuel Hibbert (1822). Alone amongst visitors, he explored Northmavine in an anti-clockwise direction. He considered the parish, "inhabited by an honest, enterprising, industrious and civil people." His description of the view from the summit of Ronas Hill is superb.

Christian Ployen (1840) the Danish governor of the Faroes arrived at Hillswick from Walls after a sixteen hour journey in a, "detestable herring boat." Fortunately he enjoyed his stay reporting that, "the scenery in Northmaven is lovely, the rocks on the west coast bold and precipitous."

John Reid (1869) a superb artist and gifted writer. "Hillswick forms an attractive centre, encircled by a galaxy of natural beauties – grotesque stacks, precipitous holms, dark tortuous caverns, combining with hill and voe to form scenes of singular and romantic interest."

Dr Robert Cowie (1871) was enchanted by walks on "beautiful soft velvety turf"" at Ure and the, "precipitous cliffs, all round, bright red colour as the Drongs at Hillswick."

John Tudor (1883) rejoiced in the, "brilliant pink stratification of the cliffs." He enjoyed his walking and gives good advice equally relevant today, "Avoid stepping on very green patches as they generally indicate quagmires, in Shetland called, "sinky places"."

Dr Mortimer Manson (1932), "The whole land is suggestive of giants and trolls and makes walking a matter of interest and excitement."

Iain Anderson (1939), "Hours and days may be spent in a boat or on moor yet no one who visits Hillswick ever seems to have done everything they wanted to do or seen all the places they wished to see, for Hillswick is only a little place in a great countryside."

Derek Gilpin Barnes (1943) strode out with two companions to escape, if briefly, the war and barrack block life of the RAF Station Sullom Voe and wondered, "in what divergent ways each man of us reacted to the ghost-ridden loneliness of that far island. Did the brooding spirits of the ancient gods whisper to my companions as they did to me? Was that thin silence shattered, in the quiet of their minds, by the clash of remote Scandinavian swords or the grinding of Norse keels upon those forgotten sands?"

Al Alvarez (1983) visited SullomVoe researching for his book 'Offshore - A North Sea Journey'. "The eerie, silent emptiness of the terminal," made quite an impression on him. "There did not even seem to be much difference between the vast unpeopled terminal shut away in Sullom Voc and the trows hidden in the hills. Although the terminal has transformed the economy of the islands, it has altered their emptiness very little. It is as if the Shetlands had their own magic that swallows up people as it has swallowed up trees leaving a green and temperate desert of grass and peat and rock, and the sea waiting wherever you turn."

Jill Slee Blackadder (2003) highlights Heylor, Ronas Voe, "a strenuous but superb walk begins here, following the massive headland past the empty crofts of Sannions and Sumra right round to the point at The Faither ..."

Today the red rocks, precipitous cliffs, hills and voes all remain visible; giants and trolls, trows and brooding spirits of ancient gods can no doubt be summoned in the imagination by us all.

WALKING IN NORTHMAVINE

A cautionary tale and a reminder to take map and compass, be properly attired and well equipped to face all weathers.

"I left Hillswick one evening and walked the distance of forty miles to Lerwick in about twelve hours. On my return two nights after, at Voe, eighteen miles from Lerwick, where two roads meet, I took the wrong one, and had walked eight miles when I overtook a solitary traveller who informed me of my blunder. Thinking to take a short cut over the hills, I left the road and climbed along the hillside. I crossed bogs where I sank knee-deep, and had to pick my way through lonesome glens. The wind blew so fiercely as almost to drive me to my wits end. I arrived at Brae (where I expected to arrive on Saturday evening) at three on the Sabbath morning; but, not having the heart to rouse the good folks there at such an untimely hour, I passed on, en route for Hillswick. On nearing my destination the cottagers, now astir, stared at me inquisitively. I fancied, from my staggering walk, that they would consider me either drunk or demented; but learned afterwards that they surmised me to be an aged clergyman on his way to the manse.

At a little past nine, after a fifty six miles walk, I had the felicity of breakfasting once more with my kind friends at Hillswick."

John T Reid 'Art Rambles in Shetland' 1869

ORDNANCE SURVEY MAP

Explorer 469 Shetland Mainland – North West; North Roe and Sullom Voe covers all walks in this book.

WALK 1: MAVIS GRIND – MANGASTER ▬▬▬▬▬▬▬▬

5 miles (8 kms) : 3 hours

Cycle/Car: Car to Mangaster, cycle to Mavis Grind, 2 miles (3 km)

OS Maps: Explorer 469 Shetland Mainland – North West

A great introduction to the Northmavine trek with no difficult terrain on this enjoyable stroll which includes prehistoric house sites.

The approach to Mavis Grind is heralded by the mighty cliff face of a quarry on the left of the road and the North Sea waters of Shetland's largest Voe, Sullom Voe on the right. When the sea is visible on both sides of the road Mavis Grind (meaning 'gate of the narrow isthmus') has been reached. Many have tried to throw a stone from the North Sea to the Atlantic, but the attempt is not recommended as it is further than it looks and a thrown stone could easily upset a passing motorist. The playwright George Bernard Shaw thought that a channel should be cut through the grind and the force of the tides passing through utilised to drive turbines.

Here a former walker viewed the prospect of "hard tramps through moors, hills and rocks" and another found that the wind was so furious that it blew his hat away beyond hope of recovery, "an extraordinary day for summer".

Cross over the wire fence and climb round a hillocky stone slope of Virdins Hill to left of a quarry. On the south facing slope of the hill there were probably three prehistoric houses. One Late Bronze Age/Early Iron Age oval house was excavated in 1978/79. Many and varied types of stone artefacts and over three thousand pottery sherds were found. Steeply descend to the small voe which features the small island of Culsetter and salmon cages. This voe is unnamed; it has been suggested that the inlet could have been dry land at the time of prehistoric settlement because the sea had yet to rise to its present level. Not known by early settlers, it remains 'Innominate Voe'.

Mavis Grind.

Walk 1: MAVIS GRIND – MANGASTER

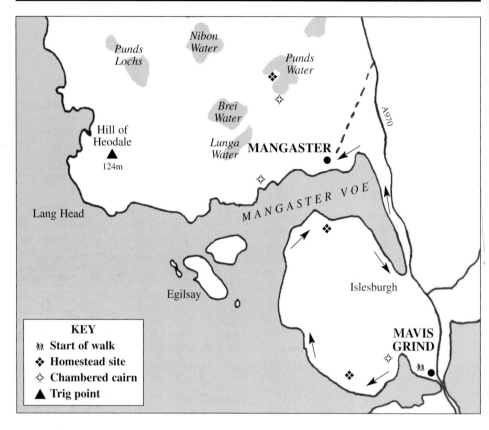

Cross the burn and ascend a gentle slope passing a shed and over a wire fence. Descend to a sheep enclosure near which are the remains of a heel-shaped cairn near the shore. The cairn has been excavated and two roughly chipped stone implements were found. A small passage led between a pair of upright stones 3ft high into a rectangular chamber. The floor of both passage and chamber was paved.

Further along, close to the shore near the Minn, is a Stone Age house-site (OS 'Homestead'). A planticrub (a drystone dyke, often circular, for the raising of young vegetable plants) is built in the hollow centre of the ruin, which is well defined outside the crub on the north by a stoney bank 2ft in height. At varying distances

around the site a massive boundary wall runs from shore to shore, roughly U shaped. It is built of drystone, is 5ft thick and 5ft high in places. The Society of Antiquaries' report comments, "None of the other house-sites is surrounded by a wall of such stoutness as this one". From the tarn above no house is visible, but on a good day the island of Foula will stand out on the far horizon.

Descend to pass three more lochs (whooper swans in winter) and appreciate the first coastal feature of this walk, where the burn from the lochs makes for the sea at the Geo of Gunavalla. There is a single stone cairn on the hill above but the view to the west across South Sound is dominated by Black Skerry and the islands of Egilsay which has a deep cliff – 'a perpendicular vein of greenstone' – which divides it into two unequal parts. Legend tells that two brothers agreed to share this island as part of their inheritance through the use of a wooden measuring device which was unequally divided within. One man, however, was blind and did not know that his brother filled the larger part of the measure for himself to ensure that it was weighted very much in his favour when turned.

"You have now your share of the money," said the heir, whose eyes were perfect. "I doubt it," said the blind one, "and may the Lord divide Egilsay to-morrow, as you have divided the money today!" The defrauded brother had his wish.

After a horrible night of thunder and lightning, the island was found in the morning split across by a deep rent into two parts, one of which, the defrauded man's share, was just twice the size of the other!

Descend to a fence and climb round the heathery hill of Too Brek and so down to a ruined wall on the shoreline. There is a large boulder and a fence and then it is into an area which can be very boggy. It is rich soil and OS shows two 'homesteads' sites here. Both were Neolithic oval houses; the first has the remains of a wall and paved floor, the second is now only a hollow 2ft deep surrounded by a bank. Pass a ruined stone enclosure and over two fences to reach the shingle beach below Islesburgh. There is the outline of a broch site east of the croft buildings. It had an overall diameter of 58ft. No stonework is now visible.

In 1953 John Copland discovered a small boulder with possibly a 1500-year-old carving on it, about 150yds to the south-west of this broch site. It was set 18 inches below ground level. A plaster cast of the carving, which measured 8 inches wide and 7½ inches high, was made and taken for further investigation in Edinburgh. It is thought to be a fanciful creation of a Pictish or Viking artist, a carving unique and peculiar to Shetland, of an eagle, probably an erne (sea-eagle). The eagle lives

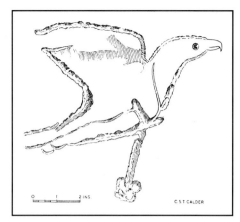

The Islesburgh Eagle.

on as the emblem of the Islesburgh Community Centre in Lerwick. The centre opened in 1946 in the magnificent Islesburgh House, built in 1907 as a residence for a merchant, Andrew Smith, who named it after this area of Northmavine because it was the property of the original Smith family.

It will have taken about 1½ hours to ramble round the coastline to this point and there is merit in crossing the burn to pass the jetty area for the salmon farmers and ascend the track to the main road.

After the end of the first crash barrier pass over a gate and descend left to discover a ruined water mill near a small burn. A larger burn flows out from a pipe under the road and we, and the burn, make for the valley floor where on the other side of two fences a very fine burn, the Burn of Mangaster, is fed from a chain of three lochs, Sinna, Glussdale and Johnnie Mann's and lazily wends its way past ruined stone buildings set on rich meadowland complete with a stone clearance cairn.

The crofts of Mangaster have a fine view of the voe, and as Dr Mortimer Manson said of this area, "the tramping is glorious among the lochs and over the hills – but the chief beauty spots are in the voes". Boats lie up on the beach. On a headland stands the ruin of an old byre enjoying a fine view: certainly the tranquility of Mangaster Voe has a lot to commend it.

WALK 2: MANGASTER – NIBON

5 miles (8 kms) : 3 hours

Cycle/Car: Car to Nibon, cycle to Mangaster, 5 miles (8 km)

OS Maps: Explorer 469 Shetland Mainland – North West

No difficult terrain on this delightful walk which includes dramatic cliff scenery and attendant stacks, geos and natural arches. Note a particularly fine, large, stone cairn which has been built on Lang Head.

On this walk from Mangaster heading west we are quickly reminded of prehistoric settlements which we will find on the way.

On the hillside at Gruna Vird, about 250 yards north west of the croft buildings of Mangaster, is a much ruined 'heel-shaped' cairn. Some

large stones remain but the chamber is now almost completely destroyed. If time allows head north to Punds Water where the best surviving heel-shaped cairn on Mainland Shetland will be found. On the north bank of the loch is another ruined, chambered cairn. (also see Circular Walk A)

Ascend to cross a dry stone wall. One can either keep the high ground to follow the stone wall or descend to cross the deep chasm of Gill Burn and make for the Pund of Mangaster. Here there is a house but no road. Climb on to

---

Walk 2: MANGASTER – NIBON

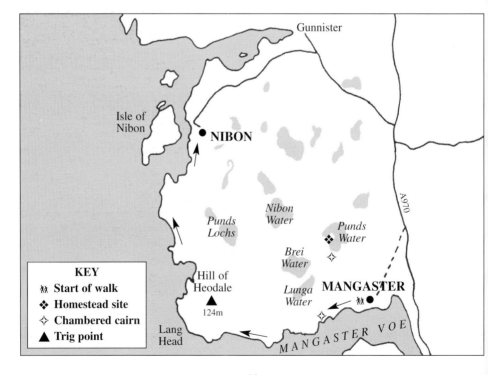

16

Punds Water heel-shaped cairn.

the heathery slopes across a wire fence and
descend again, past two small stone enclosures
and a stone cairn, into Heo Dale. Cross this to
round Heodale Head keeping an eye open for
the possible site of a medieval chapel. There is
a pund on the cliff edge – could this be it?
There are enough stones lying around to build
a cathedral. Climb the knoll to look over North
Sound and enjoy a view of Egilsay from that
point. Further along descend to a small stone
ruin above a geo opposite Black Skerry of
Ramnageo and climb to meet our first 'stone
man' on this journey.

A 7ft high lichen covered stone cairn
dominates the view and 300yds north a second
one with the stunted remains of another west
of it. Miedes to help guide sailors into
Mangaster Voe? Suddenly the walk takes on a
fresh aspect – there are wide vistas from Lang
Head and for the first time The Drongs and
Esha Ness come into view far to the north.

Higher in the hill is an L shaped 6ft by 3ft wall
with a small cairn to the south east of it and the

Cairn at Lang Head.

spot height (124m) of Hill of Heodale above. Pass the Eina Stack to descend to the sea tossed amphitheatre of Mill Geos. Natural arches abound in this easily the most dramatic stretch of coastline between Mangaster and the Ness of Hillswick. There is a good view from the stone cairn between the cliffs and Punds Lochs (whooper swans in winter).

North of Moo Stack the St. Magnus Bay Hotel at Hillswick is visible. At South End, opposite the southern part of Isle of Nibon, are the extensive ruins of a croft. Cross two burns and ascend slightly into the hill to admire an excellent waterfall, all the more dramatic for being so unexpected.

Join a wire fence as it makes its way over a burn and descend into the delightful sheltered haven of Nibon. There are a scattering of, mainly occasional, dwellings among the rocky terrain – the area has attracted habitation because the islands of Nibon and Gunnister give it some protection from the weather. The most striking dwelling is the Captain's House, built by Captain Bigland, which proudly stands at the road end.

WALK 3: NIBON – URAFIRTH ▬▬▬▬▬▬

9 miles (15 kms) : 5 hours

Cycle/Car: Car to Urafirth, cycle to Nibon, 7 miles (11 km)

OS Maps: Explorer 469 Shetland Mainland – North West

Enjoyable tramping round the voes of Gunnister and Hamar before completing the walk in protected Ura Firth. It would need a trip to Edinburgh, however, to see the Gunnister Man.

Leave Nibon heading north and as one proceeds north west to Gunnister, initially along the coast but inevitably joining the road near a salmon farm slipway, one becomes aware of how many abandoned dwellings there are. Just before a cattle grid descend left over a gate and pass by the ruins of an extensive crofting settlement, to the burn below Gunnister.

In May 1951, on the south side of the road to Gunnister, a quarter of a mile from the junction with the main road, James Bigland and James Johnson discovered the fully clothed body of a man. He was stretched out on his back in a shallow grave (only 30" deep in peat of 4ft depth above rock), his head towards east south east. There was scarcely anything of the body left but all the woollen clothing, by now in various shades of brown, was well preserved – a cap, jacket, coat, breeches and stockings as well as his belt. Inside the breeches was a small horn and a knitted purse containing some silk ribbon and three late 17th century coins of low value, one Swedish and two Dutch. A birch stick lay across his legs and at his feet was a

Orbister – place of prehistoric settlement.

Walk 3: NIBON – URAFIRTH

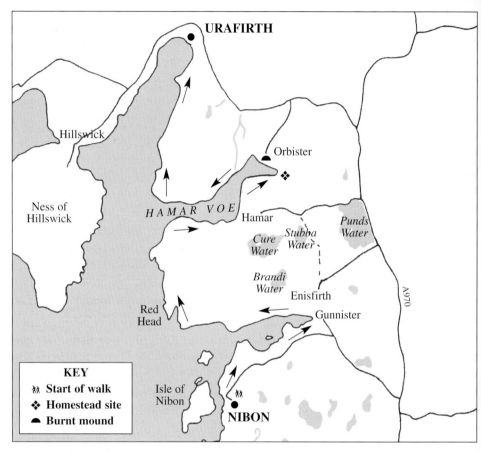

URAFIRTH

Hillswick

Orbister

Ness of
Hillswick

HAMAR VOE

Hamar

Cure
Water

Stubba
Water

Punds
Water

Brandi
Water

Enisfirth

A970

Red
Head

Gunnister

KEY
- 𖾚 **Start of walk**
- ❖ **Homestead site**
- ▲ **Burnt mound**

Isle of
Nibon

NIBON

---

small pine wooden tub, a wooden knife handle and two tablets of wood. (see photograph page 73)

Who was the Gunnister man? Could he have been a journey man? Was he the legendary murdered laird of Ure? The mystery excited much attention and most experts agreed that the man perished in wintry weather near where he was found. He was perhaps buried only on being discovered later in the year. The implements with him could indicate that he was a clerk of some sort with a portable writing desk and quill. The 300-year-old mystery remains.

The northern shore of Gunnister Voe is best traversed by following convenient sheep tracks up the hill above the ruin of Setter of Enisfirth. Five square planticrubs stand on the sheltered slope and by staying high above Silvi Geo reach a lichen covered 3ft high stone cairn by which I was once startled by the sight of a white rabbit running through the heather. Fortunately it didn't stop to take a watch from its waistcoat pocket.

Descend to follow the coastline round to Red Head. What a memorable feature this is – both in its colour and the stone arch across its cave. It marks the opening of Ura Firth and the view west includes the lighthouse near Baa Taing on Ness of Hillswick. Beware the chasm as one goes round the geo to get a closer view of the Red Head. Above Riva more stone cairns guide one on round to the Ness Head of Hamar. One cannot, however, splash across Hamar Voe to get onto Urafirth, one has to go right round it. Cross the burn by a ruined stone building below the West Mill Loch and on past the large croft of Hamar. On the shoreline are the remains of a herring station stone jetty and a modem salmon farm slip-way and shed.

A little gate in a wire fence leads one through to a shingle beach at the head of the voe. Sadly the footbridge over the burn below a small derelict house is down but the burn is leapable – just.

Between the burn and the tree-sheltered mansion of Orbister is an area of ancient settlement. A favoured spot, it attracted early habitation – evidence of a prehistoric homestead is visible here as well as our first 'burnt mound' on the Northmavine trek. About 150yds from the shore, north of the burn, it measures 9.1m long x 7.3m broad x 0.9m high.

Above, on the hillside of Olnesfirth at a site known locally as 'The Cumlins' is an irregular grass-covered cairn of loose stones said to have been a massive structure at sometime in the distant past. In 1935 several ancient hammer-stones and some pieces of pottery were unearthed. Of the broch of Orbister, said to have occupied a site at the mouth of the Burn of Eelawater, there is no trace because of the effects of coast erosion.

Perhaps the most interesting feature is the planticrub which has been built utilising a massive boulder. Within its shelter trees defiantly 'hold the fort'. A green road runs to the rear of Orbister house. Go up the road to modern sheep fold. Turn left and descend bank to cross the burn on a slatted wooden foot-bridge. 200 yards upstream is a ruined water mill. Climb up the steep slope of the Ness of Olnesfirth between Scarpy and North Lees, crossing the road and aiming west to stay above South Lees. The walk remains rugged

Orbister – tree growing planticrub.

until, after Valla Dale, ascend to finish the walk by taking the higher ground of Stugger Hill.

Descend into the welcome haven of Urafirth, a sheltered village scattered around the head of the voe where the local primary school was established over 100 years ago.

If staying the night here, better to be aware of Low's warning; he, on the 21st July, 1774, "Called at Uriefirth, a house so remarkably situated as to be in continual danger from thunder, It has been struck several times, and everything of glass shivered in ten thousand pieces, spirits dried up in casks and glasses. The house stands opposite to a valley formed by two opposite hills and seems in the way of the current of lightning, which subjects it so often to this inconveniency".

Otter making fast tracks at Nibon.

21

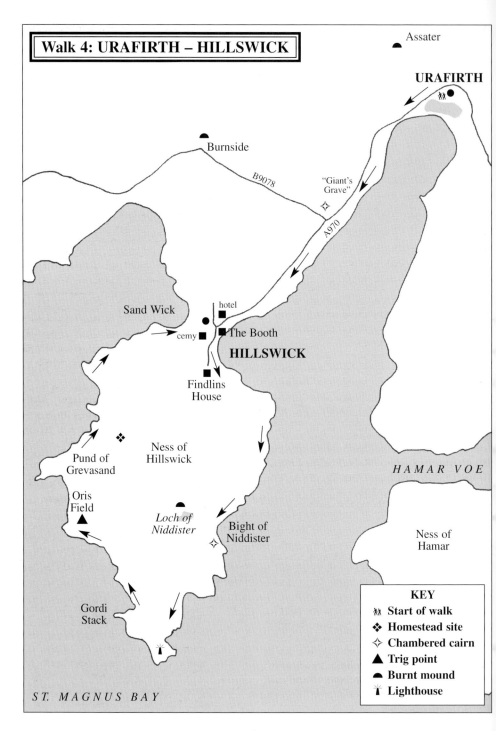

Walk 4: URAFIRTH – HILLSWICK

Assater

URAFIRTH

Burnside

B9078

"Giant's Grave"

A970

Sand Wick

hotel

cemy ■The Booth

HILLSWICK

Findlins House

Ness of Hillswick

HAMAR VOE

Pund of Grevasand

Oris Field ▲

Loch of Niddister

Bight of Niddister

Ness of Hamar

Gordi Stack

ST. MAGNUS BAY

KEY
🚶 **Start of walk**
❖ **Homestead site**
✧ **Chambered cairn**
▲ **Trig point**
● **Burnt mound**
🕯 **Lighthouse**

WALK 4: URAFIRTH – HILLSWICK ████████████

8 miles (13 kms) : 4 hours

Cycle/Car: Car to Hillswick, cycle to Urafirth, 2 miles (3 km)

OS Maps: Explorer 469 Shetland Mainland – North West

In this section of the walk there is much to be explored, much to be savoured. The timing is arbitrary. On a day of good weather one could easily spend more than the 3 hours suggested to appreciate the Ness of Hillswick. The area cannot be rushed; a longer stay in the Hillswick area will probably be necessary.

Leave Urafirth either by following the road or leaping the burn and crossing the spit of land which encloses the loch. It is on this water that the Northmavine Up-Helly-A' galley goes to its spectacular fate by fire each February. If leaving by road, and by now a burnt mound buff, turn right to Assater where about 200yds south from the houses, one will be found measuring 0.7m high.

Back on the road to Hillswick there are many fences on the low lying ground between the road and sea shore so one is well advised to use the road. The new primary school has been built here. At Gateside, to the left of a modern house with red tiled roof, about 200yds up the slope, the other side of a wire fence, is one of Shetland's more accessible heel-shaped cairns. Once known locally as 'The Giant's Grave' there are about forty small scattered boulders of the local granite with a cist positioned inside them.

The facade, which faces almost due east, is represented by nine boulders, eight fallen and one erect, set along an arc the chord of which measures 45ft.

Proceed along the road, passing on the left first Hillswick Public Hall and then a delightful traditional croft house with white walls and red roof, the Coast Guard rescue hut and, nearly opposite the church, a small building decorated with shells. It is worth admiring the artistic use of the shells by the late Johnny Harrison in the 1970s.

The church has a Gothic front, was built in 1870 at a cost of £1,700 and is dedicated to St. Magnus. Alongside it stands the handsome, wooden St. Magnus Bay Hotel. Originally pre-fabricated in Norway for use in Glasgow for the Great Exhibition of 1896, it was purchased by the North of Scotland and Orkney and Shetland Steam Navigation Co. and re-erected at Hillswick in 1902. Inclusive holidays from Leith combining the cruise on a steamer with a week at Hillswick could be enjoyed when the weekly terms at the hotel, in 1908, were £3 3s 0d! Between the wars, a cruise and a week at Hillswick cost £12 10s 0d. The withdrawal of the ship *St. Ninian* and all services from Leith in February 1971 meant the end of traditional cruises to Orkney and Shetland and that year the hotel was sold by the shipping company.

The road left opposite the hotel takes one down past the Hillswick Post Office and General Store to the foreshore and what was Shetland's oldest pub, 'The Booth'. The list of licensees once displayed in the bar went back to 1698. For over a decade Jan Morgan has run Da Bod Café specialising in vegetarian food and raising funds to look after seals and otters in the adjacent Hillswick Wildlife Sanctuary.

Tudor thought that, "to the painter, the geologist and the mineralogist, Hillswick will afford such a centre from which to follow their respective pursuits as will be hard to find elsewhere on British soil".

We should aim south east for the Ness, proceeding round the 10ft high garden wall of The Booth and looking into the old walled burial ground. This was established on the site of the medieval chapel site dedicated to St. Gregory. In 1733 another church was built a short distance away to be replaced by the present St. Magnus. On entering the burial ground metal gate two decorated memorial stones will be found built into the wall on the right and one on the left. Both date post-1707.

In 1870, in a kitchen midden near this site, were found four long-handled bone weaving combs (now in the National Museum) and remains of roe and red deer dating from the Iron Age.

The big house on the left with red granite blocks in its garden walls is The Manse. Above it are Findlins House and on the right, complete with horses and carts, is The Smithy and behind it Findlins Farm. The nearby bay is a good place to spot an otter. The terrain is usually quite marshy and it only improves after a fence has been crossed and a little height gained. At Tur Ness the sea has bored a hole

through the cliff to create a rock pool and there is a larger version a little further on at the end of a row of boulders marking a sheep pund.

At Leadie is a large stone enclosure and a sheep wash; a little further on is a small stone ruin with a small double cave in the cliff below.

Where the burn runs down from the loch to the Bight of Niddister are the remains of a water mill and small stone ruin. Follow the burn 300yds onto the plain and on a point of a low promontory at the west end of the Loch of Niddister is a crescentic burnt mound measuring 1.7m long, 14m broad and 1.7m high with two boulders on its north west slope. Apart from their uses in cooking and sauna bathing it has also been suggested that they

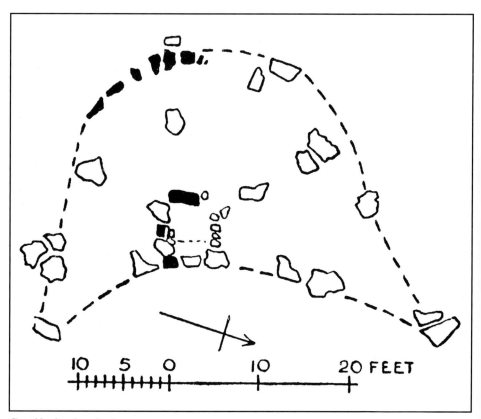

Gateside chambered cairn.

may have been used in early woollen textile production, which requires heat and moisture for the fulling process. Fulling is the means of cleansing, shrinking and thickening cloth. Considering how many sheep have been farmed in Shetland, a link to cloth processing with some burnt mounds is not improbable. Our ancestors needed clothes here as anywhere else and also, presumably, laundering facilities.

The remains of a prehistoric cairn are visible at HU 280755. Severely mutilated it stands on a low ridge about 50ft above the sea at the Bight of Niddister. Within the cairn are two blocks and some slabs suggesting the remains of a chamber.

At the next burn, down the cliff by a stone ruin, run some steps to a jetty, once used by boats servicing the lighthouse. Commence the climb above a natural arch and quaintly named The Quilse islet. It's a bit of a haul above the sweep of Queen Geos. Descend along the magnificent cliff battlements – The Drongs come into view for the first time – and approach the lighthouse on Baa Taing by following a regimented black and white column of fence posts. The lighthouse marks the entrance to Ura Firth and many a ship must have been glad to leave the turbulent waters of St. Magnus Bay by passing it, the winking light well to port.

The west coastline of the Ness of Hillswick is most dramatic. The massive Gordi Stack, which Tudor thought, "from one point of view represents a rhinoceros horn", can be appreciated from three vantage points, with the 'rhino view' being the middle one.

The cliffs are precipitous and great care is needed on leaving a view of the stack as one is walking up a deceptive slope of the hill, unaware of the long drop awaiting the unwary. Descend to pass over a stone wall with boulders, set like Fetlar's famous Finniegirt,

and climb to the spot height of Oris Field. This is on a knoll, the stones of which show traces of whitewash and two theodolite holes. Descend to the Pund of Grevasand where there is an excellent view of Isle of Westerhouse and The Drongs – in a heavy sea the water slices through its arches with such fury one is amazed the feature has survived for so long. One can walk out along the pund by stepping over a stone wall but keep down on the northern slope and be warned – this peninsula also comes to an abrupt end!

If one now turns round and heads east up onto the highest hill behind, there is a granite pyramid on the flat area on top – is this the "red unhewn obelisk of granite, mantled with grey moss, being the memorial of far remote times", that Hibbert waxed lyrical about? It's not particularly red.

Pass a cairn of stones and descend to the OS 'homestead'. This is the ruin of a Neolithic oval house, field boundaries and clearance cairns of what was an early bronze age settlement area. This example, about 60ft outside circumference, has a low oval stone and turf wall surrounding a hollow centre. There is clear evidence of the entrance on the east side

In the valley below to the north a burn runs down to the cliffs. Descend to a fence and climb to the spot height (82m), the highest point of the Ness. There are the remains of four metal stays in the concrete. Descend again, to Ber Dale and make the most of the remainder of the coastline before passing a large stone clearance cairn, piles of boulders and coming to a wall.

Follow the cliff walk outside the fence and drop down on to the pebbly beach, once particularly valued as a place for drying fish. Cross the pebbly field behind it to a gate and one is back outside The Booth once more.

WALK 5: HILLSWICK – STENNESS

9 miles (15 kms) : 4 hours

Cycle/Car: Car to Stenness, cycle to Hillswick, 7 miles (12 km)

OS Maps: Explorer 469 Shetland Mainland – North West

A walk along another stretch of dramatic cliff scenery. I hope that the sun shines onto the bold red cliffs of Grocken and The Runk. It heightens their glory to such effect that the memory of this walk particularly will never dim. It will be difficult, however, to combine this walk with a visit to the Northmavine museum at Tangwick Haa. Allow considerable 'extra time' or plan on a special visit on a 'rest day' in the area – it will be well worth it.

If you can drag yourself away from Hillswick cross the pebbly field beside the ancient walled cemetery to reach the beach of West Ayre and commence the walk round Sandwick. Climb over various field fences to view the Nista Skerries and many geos.

Hillswick – John Harrison and admirer.

Walk 5: HILLSWICK – STENNESS

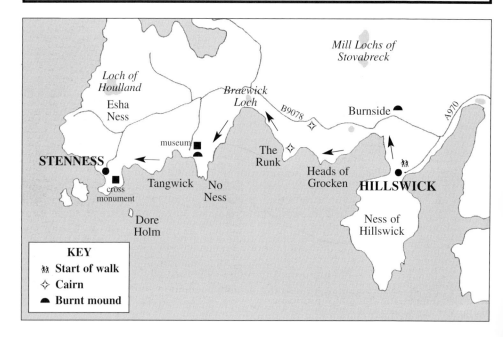

Commence the descent to the beach from Kit Geo. If the sea is at all rough there will be a magnificent sight of breakers noisily pounding the pebbles round the bay. To the south west The Drongs are visible once more. There is a wide valley behind the beach into which the burns of Dula and Stovabreck flow. Either now or later visit a most remarkable burnt mound site which is situated up the burn near the house of Burnside. Go inland and cross the road and the fence and the small twin mounds will be seen on the slope of the hill 150yds left of the burn. But what is really exciting is the sight of a surviving, complete stone cooking trough, carefully constructed of large slabs of granite and sandstone. Two other slabs, possibly intended as covers, lie on each side of the trough.

The cavity measures 4ft 3in in length and 1ft 11in in width. Certainly large enough to boil large joints of meat wrapped in straw ropes or produce steam for cleaning or the fulling process.

It is classified as crescentic and measures 11m long, 8m broad and 1m high

Return to the beach and at its northern end ascend the hill, cross over the fence and crash barrier and walk on the road until one is round the deep cleft known as the Gillie Burn, which is a paradise of wild flowers in summer. Join the cliff walk by either going left of the croft or to its right and check for birdlife on Helga Water, which was alternatively once known and revered as the 'Water of Health'. This loch may also have been the haunt of a Shetland water god or nyuggel, named the Shoopiltee who, in the form of a beautiful Shetland pony, lured people to mount him, whereupon he galloped into the water and drowned his rider. So give any ponies you might encounter a wide berth. You may find a rock on the shore with a scooped out basin which previous visitors were told was used as a baptismal font when Christianity was established in Shetland.

Back to the cliffs cross a marshy area and ascend to Grey Face, a dark headland in

Burnside – cooking trough.

The Runk.

Stoura Pund looking north towards Braewick.

Grocken.

contrast to the 'bright red Heads of Grocken'. Beware of sudden precipices when distracted by such sights of rugged grandeur. Follow the cliffs above the bay over which the cairn of Watch Hill keeps vigil. This cairn is some 18ft in diameter, marked by a kerb of stones which are placed round the circumference.

Out west to sea the island of Foula could be visible. It is the twin peaks near The Runk, however, which will attract immediate attention. A cairn on the rising ground on the eastern approach to them is a good vantage point. A little lower down is a 3ft high, red standing stone. Natural arches and blow holes seem to be everywhere on the cliffs of The Neap – one specialises in sending a column of water shooting up the cliff.

By climbing onto the neck of land to the right of the peaks one has an excellent view north up the coast and an array of stacks, bravely standing like blushing, battered survivors away from the cliffs and out into the sea.

One more warning, before descending to Braewick beware a deep cleft, 22yds long, inland from the cliff edge. Sheep bones collected within it indicate how dangerous it is.

Braewick is approached past a concrete pillar, two houses and another concrete pillar serving as a footbridge over Crossabreck Burn. Braewick Loch should be there but twice last century its defences were breached and it drained into the sea (July 1935 and October 1987). When the loch drained in 1935 the timbers of an early Norwegian boat were found in the centre of it. Amongst the timbers were norse nails, wooden pegs and bones. Cross the boulders on the beach, with its noosts and ancient mangle adapted for use as a windlass and ascend to cross Mill Burn. Here there are the ruins of two water mills, one of which is right on the cliff edge. The cliffs may not be as high as those before Braewick but these too abound in arches and blow holes. It is easy going and signs of habitation are never far away – a small castellated building first in view was the Community Hall and is now a private house. From No Ness Tangwick Haa is visible. On the headland is a stone ruin and a small pebbly beach with windlass. On the W finger of the ness is a low stone ruin. Tangwick has a high sloping pebble beach. Wild iris can grow in profusion. There is a much eroded burnt mound right on the shoreline 16m long, 9.7m broad and 1.5m high.

Leave the beach to follow a road west from Tangwick Haa. This beautiful museum was originally an 18th century manor house and the family home of the Cheyne family. On display is a portrait of Captain Andrew Cheyne born 1817, killed by natives in the South Pacific 1866. He was the father of Sir William Watson Cheyne who became one of the world's foremost surgeons and lived in Leagarth, Fetlar. (See 'Walking the Coastline of Shetland. The Island of Fetlar', Walk 3). Details of everything one might want to know about Northmavine's history can be found here, from sites of former shops to shipwrecks. There is a superb collection of local artefacts permanently on display. Here Ployen found that, "a glass of toddy was refreshing after this

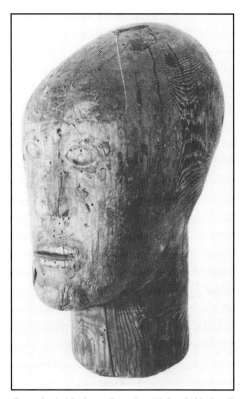

Carved wig block attributed to "Johnnie Notions" on display at Tangwick Haa Museum.
© *Shetland Museum*

fatiguing day" (he'd spent the day riding from Hillswick to Ronas Voe, crossing it, climbing Ronas Hill, returning to Hillswick and then riding to Tangwick, "in a very uncertain moonlight, and on a breakneck road"!) Sir Walter Scott also stayed here for two or three nights gathering material for his novel 'The Pirate'. On the western shore, walk in front of a large derelict booth and cross over a stone wall with a convenient step. The Houb Burn flows down to the cliffs and then cascades onto the beach below. After Gro Tang are two stone planticrubs and a first sight of the stone cross monument at Stenness. Pass a sheep wash where there is a gate in the fence and cross the burn flowing to the pebbly beach from East Loch. There is the substantial ruin of a water mill by the burn.

Cross two fences in climbing to reach the monument, which is shaped in the form of a large concrete cross on the top of the hill. It was erected in 1927 by the Commissioners for Northern Lighthouses to mark the spot where a tender could land supplies for the Esha Ness lighthouse, then being built. The splendid view from the monument also includes the offshore island of Dore Holm, a dominating feature out to sea with its famous natural arch, large enough to take a reasonably sized boat through.

Down from the monument on the south east corner of the ness is Fiorda Taing; this is a notable blow hole 60ft deep and 40ft from the edge of the cliff. On a walk renowned for arches and blow holes Dore Holm and Fiorda Taing are fitting finds near the conclusion of this stretch of coastline.

Complete the walk by going round to the south west corner of the Ness; at Utstabi was a former leper house; it is the nearest point to the protective Isle of Stenness. The derelict stone buildings are reminders of the days when Stenness was an important fishing station, and the well used by the Haaf fisherman can still be seen at the end of the beach nearest the house.

Ascend to the croft, to the side of which the main road (B9078) terminates.

WALK 6: STENNESS – HAMNAVOE ▓▓▓▓▓▓▓▓▓▓▓

8 miles (13 kms) : 6 hours

Cycle/Car: Car to Hamnavoe, cycle to Stenness, 4 miles (7 km)

OS Maps: Explorer 469 Shetland Mainland – North West

Without doubt this is one of the finest walks to be enjoyed in Shetland or indeed anywhere else. The combination of dramatic coastal scenery, unusual natural features and historical sites means that progress round Eshaness is slow. A detailed study of the kirk, broch and other prehistoric sites will require far more than the six hours allowed for this walk.

Northmavine, during the years of the Far Haaf fishing (old Norse means 'open sea') from the 1700s to the last days of the sixareen fishing boats in the 1880s, was the main ling fishing parish in Shetland. Lodges were established on beaches nearest to the fishing grounds suitable for drying the salted fish and Stenness was one of the most important. It was as near the western fishing grounds as any point of land can be with the advantage of the Isle of Stenness and Skerry of Eshaness offshore acting as breakwaters. The beach of small boulders was ideal for hauling up the boats and drying the fish between the months of May and August. Today only a busy croft remains to view the abandoned sites of the far haaf buildings and this is situated at the end of the main road. Ployen "shot a multitude of skarfs" (shags) here and ate them. This act surprised his Shetland hosts – they only used the feathers!

From Stenness beach head north west, cross a wire fence and follow the low cliffs past a stone ruin and a planticrub. Seals frequent this area and there are small natural arches to be seen.

Cross another wire fence and dilapidated stone wall to reach a shingle beach into which a burn flows from the Loch of Breckon. There were originally two water mills here; the lower one has virtually gone but the upper mill is an

excellent ruin. Across on the Isle of Stenness, kittiwakes nest on North Stole. On The Bruddans seals bask. Ascend the pebble strewn slopes past a ruined crub and decide whether to obtain a closer view of The Cannon blow hole. It involves climbing over some very slippy rocks but in the right conditions the sound and sight of it are memorable – the sea is forced out of the cave, "with a loud noise and a copious discharge of fine foam not unlike the report and smoke of a piece of ordnance", enthused Cowie.

From here follow the burn up to a dam of large boulders on the shore of Gerdie Loch. At the Wend there is a mound of stones on a spit of land. Follow the southern shore and climb the hill Sae Breck to see its trig point (61m), a disused coastguard hut and some derelict World War II defence installations complete with blast walls. The views from here are superb and the ditches of the prehistoric fort remain to remind one of the role Sae Breck has filled throughout history as a defended look-out. This is a broch site and there remains a central mound and enclosing ditch. Around it is a circular earthen bank with a diameter of 112ft from crest to crest. Nowhere more than 2ft high it is thought the bank was once much higher because the debris extends over a 16ft width.

Below, north west, is the site of the medieval Cross Kirk, some sections of its wall still standing nearly 4ft high in the Eshaness burial ground. It was dedicated to the Holy Rood and was traditionally one of the principal chapels of pilgrimage in Shetland.

Cowie describes how the snails living in the derelict kirk walls were "collected, dried, powdered and prescribed as a remedy for jaundice". And on Candlemas (2nd February)

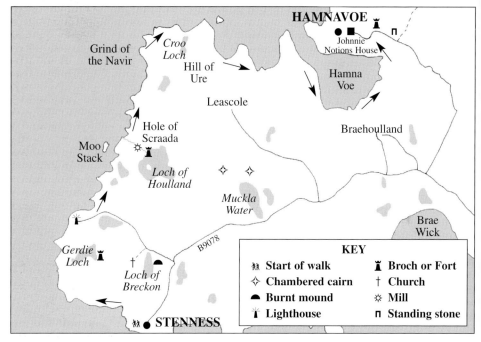

KEY

𐤊𐤊 Start of walk   𝐈 Broch or Fort
✧ Chambered cairn   † Church
◖ Burnt mound   ☼ Mill
𝐈 Lighthouse   ⊓ Standing stone

it was customary to walk to the chapel ruin at dead of night with lighted candles, which were duly solemnized and kept to be lit at future times, "whenever thunder was heard or the malevolence of demons was apprehended". This tradition so upset a minister of Northmavine, it is said that he arranged for the old kirk to be destroyed.

Cross Kirk, Eshaness. Donald Robertson's grave.

One memorial of certain notoriety will be found on the right hand side of the entrance path in front of a seventeenth century 5ft long heraldic memorial. A transcript of the lettering on the tomb is printed on a display board and reads: "Donald Robertson, born 4 January 1783. Died 4 June 1842. Aged 63 years. He was a peaceable quiet man, and, to all appearance, a sincere Christian; his death was much regretted, which was caused by the stupidity of Laurance Tulloch in Clothister who sold him nitre instead of Epsom Salts, by which he was killed in the space of 3 hours after taking a dose of it." Damned from here to eternity! Tulloch, no doubt much to local relief, moved from the district and opened a shop in Aberdeen in 1852.

The church was originally oblong in plan and measured 34ft 10ins from east to west by 20ft 3ins from north to south. The only opening traceable is the entrance centred in the west gable. A 17th century tomb slab with an illegible Latin text survives in the burial ground and a small bronze figurine of a horse found here has been identified as a 14th century Scandinavian scale-weight.

Below the burial ground on the shore line of Loch of Breckon at its north east end is a crescentic burnt mound 18m x 10m x 1.2m. Two helpful stiles allow one to enjoy a walk to it and round the loch.

Leave this loch to cross back over Sae Breck and return to the cliffs beyond The Cannon. The Eshaness lighthouse dominates the view; this stands 200ft above the sea and was built in 1929. The cliffs named The Slettans are high level wave cut rocks formed in an extinct volcano and opposite the south end of the lighthouse is the Kirn (Churn) O'Slettans, a deep narrow funnel with the sea boiling at its base. In stormy weather the sea has been known to shoot up the funnel and over the lighthouse. It would be a dangerous place to slip. Behind the lighthouse is a car park area and an excellent illustrated information display board on natural and historical features of Eshaness.

Proceed past some large boulders round South Head of Caldersgeo, another car park area with redundant Royal Navy notice board, and admire Calder's Geo – it is very deep. A subterranean passage connects the north side with the open sea. There are kittiwakes and fulmars in the next geo which is reached by ascending to a wall and climbing over a stile. Pass the Lochs of Dridgeo and view the massive Moo Stack, noting a leg shaped natural arch at its north end. Shortly after this, look east and when the mound of a broch is visible on the shore line of the Loch of Houlland, turn inland and walk towards it. Keep a sharp look-out for the Hole of Scraada; this is a long opening in the ground 132 yards from end to end and narrow all the way. At the base of its cliffs is a beach into which the sea flows through a subterranean passage 110 yards long. Originally there were two 'Holes' but on 9th October, 1873 a natural bridge separating the two collapsed into the void beneath, shortly after Morgan Thomason had crossed it on horseback. The burn from the Loch of Houlland bubbles down into the eastern end of the Hole with sufficient energy to have once powered three water mills.

Houlland broch.

33

Loch of Houlland, Eshaness.

The view of the mills is enhanced by the backdrop of cascading water and the broch which dominates a small promontory which juts out from the north west into the loch. It is an impressive ruin with walls on the north and north east surviving to a height of 12ft. Overall diameter is 57ft and the wall is 15ft thick. The entrance, which is at the west south west is 3ft wide at the mouth. On the right is the traditional cell or guard chamber.

Three lines of defence can be seen with an entrance passage 5ft wide running through the two outer lines and over the inner bank. At the south end of the headland the broch was connected to the adjacent island by a causeway 9ft broad. The island was connected by another causeway to the west shore of the loch – which presumably helps the sheep to graze the island.

Around the broch the sub-rectangular and oval foundation ruins of a later, possibly Pictish, settlement, have been identified.

Further inland between the Loch of Houlland and Muckla Water the OS marks two chambered cairns. The more westerly one is the March Cairn, Hamars of Houlland, which stands 5ft 6 inches high and measures 33ft 6ins

from north west to south east and 34ft 6ins from north east to south west. This cairn, a square example of a heel-shaped type, is a puzzle to the archaeologists because, against the general pattern, its chamber was entered by a passage which opened from the eastern side, and this side did not have a facade. (see plan below)

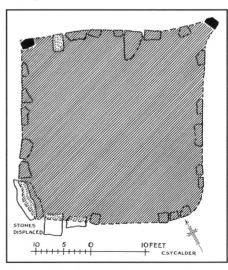

Hamars of Houlland, chambered cairn plan.

34

Return to the cliffs at Scraada and cross stiles over the wire fences to reach the fertile plateau named the Villians of Ure. The green turf stretches for over a mile along the coast and about half a mile inland.

The cliffs abound in caves and natural arches, the rocks ceaselessly scarred by the violence of the waves. One prominent stack, 200ft offshore and about 300ft high, is the Maiden Stack. After passing Gruna Stack comes the Grind of the Navir ('gate of the borer'), a natural feature which has attracted attention above all other on Eshaness.

The Atlantic has found a weak spot in the cliff face and smashed through it leaving the vertical sides of the breach open to view and smoothed by the action of the waves. The breach is 36ft wide with a lower step 40ft above the sea. The sides are 45ft in height. Behind it is a basin of about 90ft in diameter filled with water. Huge cubical blocks of rock rise from the edge of the basin; the blocks have been torn from the cliffs and driven back into the breach. It is possible to descend through the gateway to view the sea between the high rock walls.

Red rocks predominate whether on the Head of Stanshi or in the large dilapidated walls of the sheep pens on the cliffs nearby. At the point and stack of The Burr is a boulder-strewn foreshore between the sea and Croo Loch; a small roofless building sits on the loch's west shore and beside the burn flowing into its south end is a ruined water mill. Ascend the slopes of the Hill of Ure to view Shalder Sound and many seals basking on the reef of rocks named the Targies. Away out to sea north the natural arch through the offshore island of Muckle Ossa is visible. On the Hill of Ure at North House is a medieval chapel site and burial ground. The chapel building was traditionally associated with a croft out-building situated on a small knoll but 'kirkure' has long since disappeared.

There are burns to be crossed at the Geo and the boggy Dale of Ure on the slopes of which stands a solitary crub in the shape of a 4ft high tower. Descend to the headland of Raasmi where there are seven stone enclosures of various shapes and sizes.

We are now entering Hamna Voe, another notable fishing station in the past and a salmon

Grind of the Navir, Eshaness.

cage maintains a tradition today. From a marshy area a burn flows to the foreshore with two crubs by it. Upstream is a derelict water mill with two surviving mill stones. Other signs of past activity are an abandoned croft, four more planticrubs and three ruined stone fishing lodges on the cliff edge. Follow a fence down past a derelict Haa, with two standing stones in its garden, and a croft, before crossing the sandy beach of Cross-voe-sand. Over the road leading to the salmon farm jetty is a stile to help one on the way to Hoohivda. Beside this croft a fast flowing burn runs under a well constructed footbridge and artist Paul Whitworth has established a studio gallery here.

Follow the foreshore below Scarff passing a planticrub still enjoying active service. About 150yds from the shore north of the inner end of Hamna Voe on the west bank of the burn is a crescentic shaped burnt mound 1 metre high.

Cross-voe-sand standing stones.

Return to the foreshore and follow it to Riva Taing. There are many more ruins dating from the days of the fishing station here. The walk round Hamna Voe is now complete. Walk up the slope to the main area of settlement, all enjoying commanding views and seek out the house which today stands in the area traditionally associated with John Williamson, known as 'Johnny Notions', who developed an effective inoculation for smallpox in the 18th century.

He was born about 1740 at the period of history when Shetland suffered long plagues of smallpox; recurrent from 1700 to 1800 every twenty years, it devastated the island populations. Williamson devised a serum and inoculated over 3000 people without apparently losing a single patient. He died here in 1804 and was buried in the cemetery at Cross Kirk, Breckon.

At that time in England Dr Edward Jenner was working on his smallpox inoculation and its success eventually led to the more public and universal recognition of his work. John Williamson, according to a medical authority, "deserves to be held in high regard ... his pursuit of a remedy to this dread disease (smallpox) remains an intellectual tour de force." A camping bod offering accommodation has been established at a house associated with 'Johnnie Notions'.

Another of Northmavine's famous sons, Dr Tom Anderson MBE, 1910-1991, was also born and buried in Eshaness. He wrote over 500 tunes and taught hundreds to play the fiddle. He also collected and preserved Shetland fiddle tunes and is credited with the revival of traditional Shetland music. As a boy he was taken to Lerwick for the first time by his father. At the Market Cross he was captivated by the playing of George Stark, 'Da Blind Fiddler'. Tammy later recounted in the 'Shetland Folk Book', "He wis my God for da time bein". In the 1960s he formed the Shetland Fiddlers and later Shetland's Young Heritage, a group of young fiddlers who became internationally famous. The group played at his funeral one of his famous tunes,

Dr Tom Anderson with Shetland's Young Heritage, 1983.

'Da Slockit Light'. In 1970 he recalled during an interview: "I was coming out of Eshaness in late January, 1969, the time was after 11pm and as I looked back at the top of the hill leading out of the district I saw so few lights compared to what I remembered when I was young. As I watched, the lights started going out one by one. That, coupled with the recent death of my late wife, made me think of the old word 'Slockit', meaning, a light that has gone out, and I think that was what inspired the tune."

Further down the main road is the Eshaness Post Office and on the left cross over a field fence to view the broch. It is noteworthy because of its position and the defensive ditches which surrounded it. It was built away from the shore on the edge of a gully running north and south.

On the east side the drop into the gully, in which a stream flows, is very steep. It is the rampart on the north west however, which is the outstanding feature of this broch. It is up to 8ft tall and over 200ft long. The external diameter of the broch is 62ft and the remains of the tower are exposed on the surface at three points north west, south east and in the north east where there is stone work which was probably part of the guard chamber cell. Continue 500yds down the road and at the junction with a track going north to Tingon are two standing stones: The Giant's Stones. These two stones, on a line lying east and west, are 67ft apart. The more easterly has a pointed top and is 5ft 7ins high; the other stone is 7ft 7ins high.

In 1774 Low reported, "originally three stones, one of them now much shortened and the third broke off by the earth". The stones mark the end of this magnificent and memorable walk and for what history they have witnessed: truly one wishes, "that these stones could speak".

WALK 7: HAMNAVOE – HEYLOR ▌

8 miles (13 kms) : 4 hours

Cycle/Car: Car to Heylor, cycle to Hamnavoe via road along Ronas Voe and turning south before Skeo Head to join A970 at Urafirth, 8 miles (13 km)

OS Maps: Explorer 469 Shetland Mainland – North West

This magnificent walk includes a coastal route on pleasant terrain on cliffs of various hues and heights, with no sign of human habitation, *apart from Tingon, until Heylor is reached. After The Faither the walk requires more effort and is along the south bank of Ronas Voe. The*

Walk 7: HAMNAVOE – HEYLOR

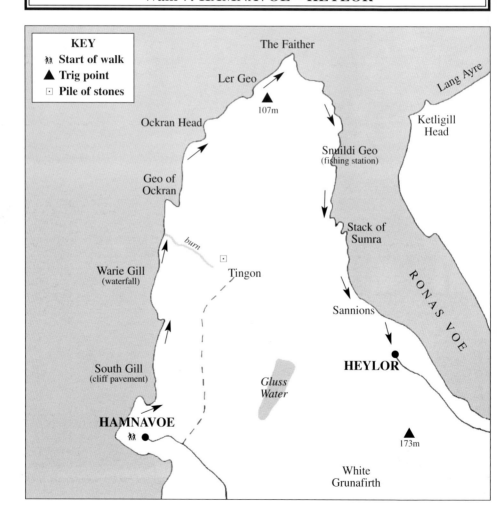

KEY
- 🚶 **Start of walk**
- ▲ **Trig point**
- ⊡ **Pile of stones**

The Faither

Ler Geo

Lang Ayre

▲ 107m

Ockran Head

Ketligill Head

Snuildi Geo (fishing station)

Geo of Ockran

Stack of Sumra

burn

⊡

Warie Gill (waterfall)

Tingon

R O N A S V O E

Sannions

South Gill (cliff pavement)

HEYLOR ●

Gluss Water

HAMNAVOE
🚶 ●

▲ 173m

White Grunafirth

voe resembles in shape a bent arm, the elbow of which pushes south towards Urafirth. Across the voe are the lower reaches of Shetland's highest hill, Ronas Hill. The cliff scenery between The Faither and the road end at Heylor is as dramatic as anywhere in Shetland and not to be missed.

Leave 'Johnnie Notion's house' at Hamnavoe and walk west down to the cliffs of Riva Taing; the land has been cultivated and there are occasional gatherings of boulders. Cross a fence to reach the boulder beach of Whal Wick where there is a view up the burn towards the broch. Cross another fence and cross a marshy boulder-strewn area with large dilapidated stone enclosures and sheep wash. Some large stones lie together resembling collapsed dolmens. The small stone ruin spotted 400yds into the hill is not a mill though there are mill lochs above. From Hoken one is on the Villains of Hamnavoe, walking is easy going. Pass a

tarn, low stone wall and another tarn. At South Gill the cliff height increases and includes black rock shelving. The burn from Punds Water cascades over the cliff.

Cross a high stone wall to ascend to Erne's House, a 4ft cairn standing on a stone pavement. There is a small tarn behind the cairn and on a hillock east of the tarn are stones set in the shape of a cist.

Tingon lies further inland and is the site of a medieval chapel but the walls of the building associated with this have completely tumbled. The wall dimensions measured 9 metres east west and 3.5 metres north south. To investigate the 'Pile of Stones' shown on the OS map walk to the Burn of Tingon where the concrete footbridge (incorporating a bedstead and bottles) has sadly collapsed but still affords a route to cross. On the slope of the hill over a fence is a striking standing stone, roughly

Hamnavoe broch.

39

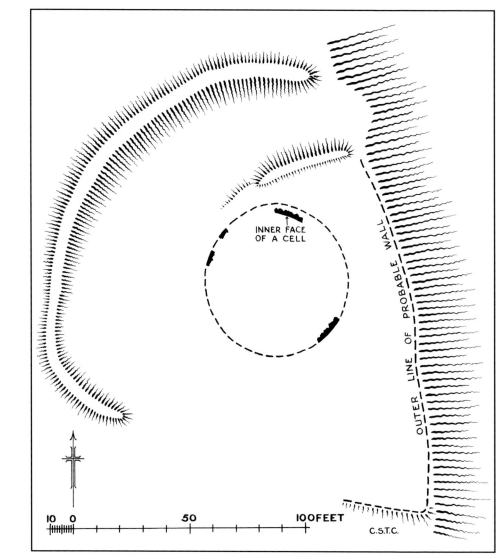

INNER FACE
OF A CELL

OUTER LINE OF PROBABLE WALL

10 0   50   100FEET

C.S.T.C.

Hamnavoe broch plan.

measuring 5ft high 8ft circumference and 2ft broad. It is angled slightly towards the west. The 'pile of stones' is just that but beyond is the ruin of a large croft. Return to the coast and the north side of Warie Gill and view two huge caves in the base of the sheer black cliff. Note a fine waterfall which is fed by the Burn of Tingon.

The eroded lava cliffs sometimes have peculiar shapes and above this Warie Gill, a lump of lava resembling the head of a camel, stares defiantly out to sea.

Below, the cliffs may be small, but still abound in natural arches. Approach Geo of Ockran past the collapsed pile of Robies Skeo.

Descend the steep slope to cross another burn which cascades over the cliff and pass outbuildings of Ockran croft. The 1851 census recorded ninety-nine inhabitants on this Ness with fourteen separate crofts. All the families were evicted and the area 'cleared' from 1865 onwards. West out to sea Little Ossa and the natural arch in Muckle Ossa are just visible. Before going up to the croft turn east and follow Mill Burn east to where it emerges from a defile; there is a ruined water mill and two small stone enclosures adjacent to it. There is also a small natural knoll similar in shape to a burnt mound. Go up to the croft passing a number of small stone clearance cairns – the ruin is substantial. It is a delightful, reasonably sheltered spot – Foula is visible south west.

The modest elevation of Ockran Head is in contrast to the height of the approaching cliffs at Gorsend's Geo which appear to be particularly bold. Climb into the hill to round the geo and from the top enjoy a dizzy view of the swirling waters beneath.

From the north side view a colony of kittiwakes and cave on the south cliff. From Bay Hevda, Uyea Isle and the peaks of the Ramna Stacks are visible. Climb up onto Clew Head and walk round dark and forbidding Ler Geo. A burn connects it to Lergeo Water, an attractive loch; mountain hares frequent the area. At the trig point (107m), a superb panoramic view: Lang Ayre east, Saxa Vord on Unst north, Foula south west. Descend onto The Faither peninsula where only a small group of boulders indicate possible previous human visitation. A final view of Muckle Ossa W and then walk round Galti Geo – perhaps after three hours exploring it's time for a break and enjoy sight of the narrow arch through Galti Stack. The spectacular scenery across the water from Ketligill Head up the coast to Hevdadale Head is a great distraction.

Proceed south east along the cliffs of Ronas Voe. On the approach to Snuildi Geo are three ruined stone buildings, like former haaf fishing lodges, on a small promontory. Four more ruins stand a little further on adjacent to large reasonably flat areas of rock. The burn from

Helia Waters tumbles down some natural steps on its way to the sea. From Geo Larradale it is a climb up Bratta Beck; cross over a fence to look down on the red stack of Sumra. Above is the ruined croft of Sumra but it will be the view of the many assorted stacks below which will command attention and in particular the shape of tall columns on the shore line. East of the ruined croft of Sannions is the Point of Quida Stack – a trunk of rock standing vertically out of the sea narrowing at its base. At Sanda Calla more strange formations and wonderful colouring – four peaks of various heights soar up from the base of the cliff whilst other stacks stand out at Weinni Neap.

Then on The Cupps pass a final bluff of rounded red rocks before descending to the settlement at Heylor, a former Haaf Fishing Station. Follow an old track over a footbridge and notice a possible mill ruin just below the bridge on the Burn of Loomishun. The houses of Heylor stretch right along the voe and the area has seen much activity in its time. At The Blade, opposite the former and much dilapidated Post Office is a substantial stone pier and skeleton of a former extension. All that is left of a former factory is a chimney with four redundant pots.

This walk ends here but if you have the energy and inclination note that above Heylor broods the Hill of White Grunafirth with its trig point (173m). It is a brisk 1.25 miles climb above the pier and the Inventory noted a group of seven large stone slabs there within about 15ft of one another. Three slabs, lying close together, marked the entrance to an underground chamber, once entered down three stone steps.

Spread the warm moonbeams gentle
shades o'er Shetland's highest hill.
Spent the storm, soon our eager
blades caress seas now still
As we pull for that peaceful shore
where bright the peat fires glow
To steer us, cheer us into Ronas voe.

'Ronas Voe' – Frank Chadwick
(1920-2006)

WALK 8: HEYLOR – NORTH COLLAFIRTH

6 miles (10 kms) : 3 hours

Cycle/Car: Car to North Collafirth (where the track goes up Collafirth Hill), cycle to Heylor, 6 miles (10 km)

OS Maps: Explorer 469 Shetland Mainland – North West

A sheltered walk, half of it along the unclassified road by the side of Ronas Voe with its own poignant memorial. Join the A970 main road as it heads north to Isbister. No climbing – that is to come in the next section!

Leave Heylor and walk east along the road. At Skeo Head turn towards the shore to the left of the Ronas Fisheries buildings and walk back west to Hollander's Ayre. About 300yds along the shore line there is a small red stone cairn with a simple plaque, 'Hollanders' Graves'.

It is the memorial to Dutch sailors killed in action in 1674 when their Dutch East Indian, *Wapen van Rotterdam* was captured by the RN frigate *Newcastle*. The Dutch vessel, like other warships were to in the 20th century, had used Ronas Voe as a shelter during one of the Anglo-Dutch Wars. The Dutch sailors are buried beneath this spot.

Continue along the road enjoying the view across the water of the slopes of Ronas Hill, mainly coloured varied shades of brown but

---

Walk 8: HEYLOR – NORTH COLLAFIRTH

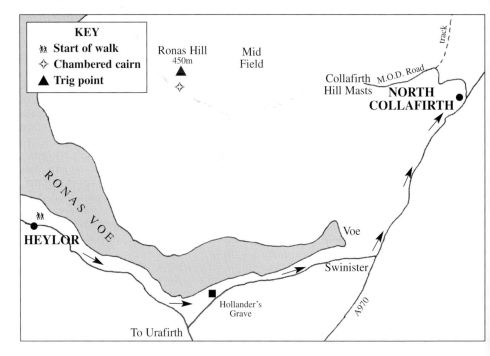

42

Ronas Voe – Hollanders' Graves.

round the derelict croft of Feal changing to green.

At one time fishermen used to collect bait from the large mussel-beds there. At the head of the voe, between 1903 and the 1920s, were two Norwegian whaling stations. Those living in Voe and Swinister enjoy their delightful locations now undisturbed by activity from this industry. Swinister is the possible location of a medieval chapel site.

Another memorial with Ronas Voe associations is not to be found here but in Lerwick. On Victoria Pier, where the main car park is, stands a red marble fountain erected in 1890 in memory of Captain John Gravill and Dr Charles Smith, and the crew to whom he was surgeon on the Hull whaler *Diana*. The *Diana* left Hull on 19th February, 1866, and with a full crew steamed out of Lerwick on 8th March and returned with seal skins in April. She left Lerwick again on 8th May with a crew of 50 for waters west of Greenland. On 2nd April, 1867 the *Diana* entered Ronas Voe with eight corpses, five of them Shetlanders, some of those who had died when the ship had got stuck in the Arctic ice. The *Diana* was the first Hull whaler to be fitted with steam engines and during her fourteen month trip had been ice bound for six months with only two month's provisions on board. Of a total ship's crew of fifty, thirteen men including the captain perished.

On the ship's arrival in Ronas Voe only two of the crew were strong enough to go aloft. The people in the area responded quickly with help and care but sadly three of the crew died on the day Ronas Voe was reached and there were three more fatalities before the *Diana* departed for Lerwick.

In 1890 Frederick Smith, at that time Mayor of West Ham and brother of Charles who had died in 1879, caused to be erected on the pierhead at Lerwick the drinking fountain, a memorial and reminder to all of "The Providential Return of the S. Whaler 'Diana' of Hull 1866-7".

The *Diana* fast in the Arctic ice, December 1869.

On reaching the A970 road at Swinister, head north along it through South Collafirth to reach the road up Collafirth Hill at North Collafirth. There is a telephone kiosk at the junction of the road to Leon and Ollaberry but the most eye-catching aspect of this district is the number of trees growing in the gardens of the various houses along the way. The great mass of Ronas Hill provides sufficient shelter for people here to take an obvious pride in their gardens. The road up Collafirth Hill is not signposted. It will be found about 100yds further north past the house called Forsa, which stands surrounded by a plantation of fir trees.

WALK 9: NORTH COLLAFIRTH – LANG CLODIE WICK ■■■■

8 miles (13 kms) : 4 hours

OS Maps: **Explorer 469 Shetland Mainland – North West**

The next section of the Northmavine trek takes us up and over Shetland's highest hill and to the most remote section of the coast. Those walking the entire route will wish to start from North Collafirth and probably aim to camp further north than Lang Clodie Wick. Those requiring accommodation can leave the coastline at Lang Clodie Wick and return to Collafirth Hill in about 3 hours. Others may simply wish to walk to the summit of Ronas Hill and return, either from the bottom of Collafirth Hill (a 3 hour round trip) or from the car park area near the radio mast buildings (2 hour round trip). In all cases be properly equipped!

Up Collafirth Hill the climb west is initially on a tarmac road, a reminder of the days when an Army signals unit was established here. Shortly after the road bends, notice a track heading north below a concrete water supply

building – it is down this track that those walking the circular route and returning from Lang Clodie Wick will complete this walk. From the bottom of Collafirth Hill it takes about half an hour to reach some masts. The Drongs are visible south west. Where the road ends at the second mast there is a turning area and a red granite cairn built by Scottish Natural Heritage. On it, under the heading 'A Walk to the Arctic', is an interpretive board highlighting the walk to Ronas Hill, the geology and plant life of this very special area. A wheeled trackway heads NW to a loose stone cairn on Man O'Scord. Before reaching the cairn on Mid Field the 'heather line' will be reached and thereafter all is bare stone. The Trig Point on top of Ronas Hill should be visible. To avoid Grud Burn walk to the north of a small tarn and Shurgie Scord and pass another cairn before reaching the cairn protected trig point at

Ronas Hill summit looking down on Trig Point and prehistoric chambered cairn.

Walk 9: NORTH COLLAFIRTH – LANG CLODIE WICK

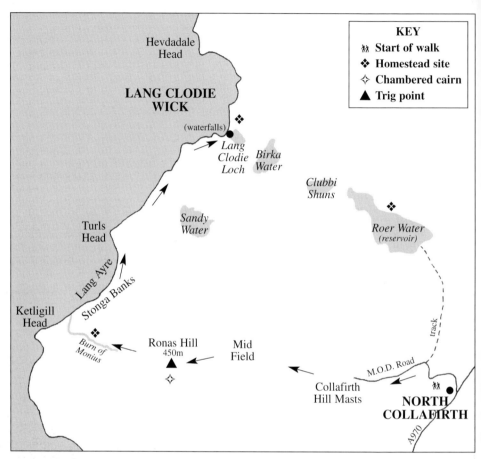

KEY
- 🏃 Start of walk
- ❖ Homestead site
- ✧ Chambered cairn
- ▲ Trig point

Hevdadale Head

LANG CLODIE WICK

(waterfalls)

Lang Clodie Loch

Birka Water

Clubbi Shuns

Roer Water
(reservoir)

Turls Head

Sandy Water

Ketligill Head

Lang Ayre

Stonga Banks

Burn of Monius

Ronas Hill
450m
▲

Mid Field

track

Collafirth Hill Masts

NORTH COLLAFIRTH

M.O.D. Road

A970

---

the summit of Ronas Hill 1475ft (450m). Time taken from the bottom of Collafirth Hill will now be about one and a half hours. Even on a day of good weather the shelter provided by the trig point cairn can be very welcome. The views can be spectacular with a sweep of about 80 miles. Both the Muckle Flugga Lighthouse, north, and Fair Isle, south, can be visible – just the place to celebrate the longest day of the year in June. However, the weather may be awful and the hood of one's anorak useful to fend off the hailstones.

A few yards west some boulders have been set in a circle with a cross in it. To the south west

is a well preserved chambered cairn which originally measured about 45ft in diameter. The single compartment chamber is reached through the entrance on the east and a passage about 5ft high. The chamber is built of massive blocks and is 4ft high, 5ft 6in long and 3ft broad. Many must have found sanctuary here over the centuries and your arrival may cause resting snow buntings, fieldfare or other sheltering birds to move on.

A snowy owl was once seen near the summit in recent years – perhaps a refugee from Fetlar. More likely to be spotted are some of the fifteen species of Arctic flowering plants which grow on the slopes. Leave the trig point to descend north west for Ketligill Head, keeping sharp look out for dangerous chasms created by fissures in the ground. Three cairns are set about half way down the slope – aim to go to the south west of the bottom one to follow the Burn of Monius. On the left bank of the burn half a mile east south east of Ketligill Head, in a dip in the hillside at an elevation of 500ft above sea-level, the Inventory notes traces of ancient buildings. Possibly the remains are those of prehistoric dwelling places or shelters but no relics have been discovered on the site to date.

The coastal features and offshore stacks of Whal Horn, The Roodrans, Cleiver and Hog may all have been spotted on Walk 7 from the west side of Ronas Voe when walking south from The Faither.

At Ketligill Head one can climb down to the beautiful long, lonely, red beach of Lang Ayre. Proceed north along the heights of Stonga Banks and enjoy a final view of the ayre from Turls Head, the approach to which involves crossing depressions in the ground resembling the defensive ditches of some ancient hill fort. On the edge of the cliff at The Crook is a metal pole 3ft high and a view of another ayre below Valla Kames. Out at sea is the largest of the sea rocks on this walk – Gruna Stack – remarkable for its caves, deep fissures and buttress-like protuberances the whole of which Dr Manson likened to the appearance of a cathedral.

It is fine cliff walking and despite so many small lochs to the E there is only one marshy area. Above Djubi Geo climb on to the highest point of the cliff to look down on Lang Clodie Loch, the burns from it flowing over the cliff to create two magnificent waterfalls, one in the southern corner said to be the finest in Shetland. There are dramatic vertical arches through the cliffs opposite and protecting Lang Clodie Wick to the north is the splendid headland, Hevdadale Head.

Lang Ayre from the south.

47

Gruna Stack 'like a cathedral'.

Lang Clodie Wick waterfall.

Time now taken from the bottom of Collafirth Hill three and a half hours.

Cross the burn on stepping stones above the waterfall and if returning to Collafirth Hill follow the Circular I route. If equipped to do so and camping or pushing on north turn to Walk No. 10.

The OS marked 'homestead' has been described as a circular structure in scree area with a diameter of 12.2 metres. No coherent plan. Entrance to the west would indicate a possible Iron Age Round House rather than a cairn.

I have not located this site but thought I had when finding, just north of the falls, two circular buildings and a peculiar rectangular chamber 8ft long and 3ft wide roofed by blocks of granite. Remains of a neolithic motel? Perhaps the falls of Lang Clodie Wick attracted prehistoric honeymooners in much the same way as Niagara Falls attracts them today!

WALK 10: LANG CLODIE WICK – SANDVOE ███████████

10 miles (16 kms) : 5 hours

Cycle/Car: Car to Sandvoe, cycle to North Collafirth, 5 miles (8 km)

OS Maps: Explorer 469 Shetland Mainland – North West

The next stretch of the coastline walk includes dramatic coastal scenery and a visit to the island of Uyea (Øya). However, the island can only be visited when the tide is out and reliable information on tides must be obtained in advance in order to avoid the possibility of being marooned.

If you have not camped the night at Lang Clodie Wick but returned to accommodation near North Collafirth then we have to get you back here. One can return via Roer Water (route described in Circular Walk I) which adds another 4 miles (7kms) to the distance and up to three hours in time.

Those who have camped out overnight at Lang Clodie Wick may have found a site near the homestead. We can now all walk north along the coastline. Climb up and around the top of Innri Geo – a remarkable canyon – and then up the bluff of Hevdadale Head. There is a large sloping boulder on top of this magnificent headland upon which one can sit and admire the view. The waterfall from Burn of Murie is in sight. Descend north over single height stone wall to the valley of Hevda Dale. Moo Stack is in view and a natural arch through Dorra Stack off Uyea Isle. Pass a stone dyke and small stone enclosure to climb onto boulder strewn slopes of Hamara Field. There is a much delapidated, but 4ft high in places, stone wall which terminates in a circular enclosure at a fence above Cleras Geo.

From a striking large red boulder Fugla Ness and the Ramna Stacks are in view. From Tongan Swarta there are fewer boulders but the steep valley through which Brettoo Burn tumbles requires careful walking. Red Geo is very red indeed. With some relief walk on to South Wick, spotting any seals which may be on Wilma Stack, and pass a low stone

enclosure, circular sheep pen and fence. Notice caves in the cliffs above the beach. Cross two burns, one with footbridge also used by the sheep and cross a third burn near a ruined stone building. On Fugla Ness some striking red boulders but the headland is grey. There is a small cairn and the area is a haven for gulls; after Sand Geo ascend to The Ness and view Uyea Isle either across the sand bar or the sea if the tide is in. If wishing to explore Uyea isle then cross the sandy bar if the tide is well out in order to reach it. In the cliffs facing west in The Ness is Kettlebaak Cave. I have not located it and it may only be accessible with

Looking back at Lang Ayre.

49

Walk 10: LANG CLODIE WICK – SANDVOE

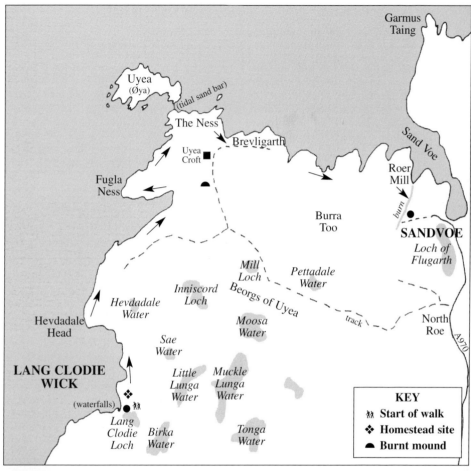

Access across a tidal sand bar to Uyea Isle.

the help of a local guide. Manson reports that, "the unique thing about this cave is the 'baak' or 'beam' formed by the natural arch right across it about two-thirds up. In the days of the press-gang this cave was a favourite hiding place, for the 'baak', which could be climbed up to, made detection almost impossible." Presumably, it is in Big Nev Geo below the cliff top, spot height (70m).

It will have taken up to two hours from Lang Clodie Wick. Uyea Isle, so beautifully green, was once reckoned to provide "one of the richest pastures for cattle". A haaf fishing station was once established at Burrier Wick and in the north west corner in 1851, there were ninety-two inhabitants. Not content with only having Skerries named after him in West Yell, Robert Irvine has another one off Uyea.

In 1701 a Dutch armed whaler, the *Duiker* was lost off Uyea and a number of her crew drowned. In 1744 another Dutch armed vessel *Abraham* was also wrecked here and survivors marooned on the isle for two days until the weather moderated. Neither *Duiker* nor *Abraham* have been located to date but a 7ft long bronze gun from *Duiker* was salvaged by local fishermen.

Neolithic axe factory, Beorgs of Uyea.

Back on the mainland walk east round the green pastures of North Wick to explore the eight ruined fishing station houses on the banks opposite Nista Skerries. The aptly named Fisherman's Loch lies just to the south. Follow the fence up and round The Breck before descending to the north east of Uyea Croft – what a splendid location it enjoys. A track goes east up North Hill terminating before the beautifully situated ruin of the croft at Brevigarth. From Calder's Head to Sandvoe the coast walk can be quite taxing if very rewarding. A more direct route involves climbing inland up marshy The Hoga and Burra Too on the north slope of Saefti Hill. Descend to cross the Burn of Sandvoe which flows into the sea at Roer Mill.

It is worth a diversion to explore down the dale to the beach at Roer Mill, where there is a ruined booth (bod), although here was once the scene of an infamous incident. In 1774 a pirate ship anchored in the Voe and, following a dispute onboard, one of the pirates, Jacob Stays, was bound hand and foot and brought ashore. Here he was murdered by being buried alive, much to the horror of the islanders who were powerless to intervene.

Return up the burn to an excellently preserved ruin of a water mill where one crosses the burn to join the track which goes down past a small loch to the small, sheltered settlement at Sandvoe. There is a sandy beach in front of the cemetery and those who have walked The Ness will cross a stile before reaching the fence at the road. Sandvoe was the birth place of James Inkster (1843-1927) author of 'Mansie's Rod', written in the old Shetland dialect. This book includes a number of stories finally published in one volume in 1922; it is considered to be one of the most realistic works written describing the old crofting life in Shetland.

51

Walk 11: SANDVOE – NORTH ROE

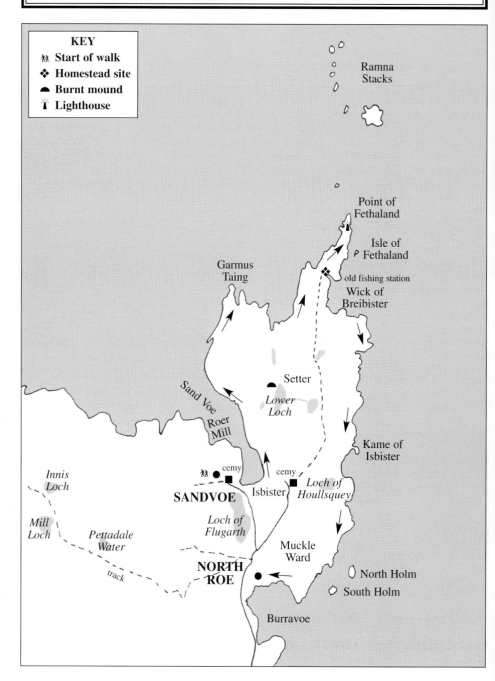

KEY
- 🚶 Start of walk
- ❖ Homestead site
- ◓ Burnt mound
- 🗼 Lighthouse

Ramna
Stacks

Point of
Fethaland

Isle of
Fethaland

Garmus
Taing

old fishing station

Wick of
Breibister

Setter

Lower
Loch

Sand Voe

*Roer
Mill*

Kame of
Isbister

*Innis
Loch*

cemy

cemy

SANDVOE

Isbister

*Loch of
Houllsquey*

*Mill
Loch*

*Pettadale
Water*

*Loch of
Flugarth*

Muckle
Ward

**NORTH
ROE**

track

North Holm

South Holm

Burravoe

WALK 11: SANDVOE – NORTH ROE ████████████████████

10 miles (16 kms) : 5 hours

Cycle/Car: Car to North Roe, cycle to Sandvoe, 1 mile (2 km)

OS Maps: Explorer 469 Shetland Mainland – North West

This walk takes us round the northern-most point of Mainland Shetland. It may be rocky in parts but no heather – green grazing land is the characteristic landscape of this area. There is a direct circular route to the Isle of Fethaland and this option is to be found in Circular Walk K. The walk includes a range of interesting historical sites, from the fishing lodges of Fethaland to the cliff settlement of the Kame of Isbister. It ends in North Roe, which is a superb base from which to explore Northmavine.

At Sandvoe go through the gate to the left of the cemetery and turn E. along the beach or

low bank and use the bridge to cross the burn. Rather than aiming for the coast below Benigarth take the track which ascends to its east and soon the Lower Loch of Setter will come into view. Below the track left is a burn flowing down from the loch to Orr Wick. There are two ruined water mills, and the mill stones from the lower mill grind on, but not here. Gifted to Tommy Isbister MBE of Trondra, he has installed them in his beautifully restored mill at Burland.

Wild iris abound. The track ends at the loch where there are the remains of a small bridge over the burn. Two burnt mounds have been

Shetland ponies, Garmus Taing.

Ruined fishing lodges, Fethaland.

identified by this loch, on the south east and north west shore at the top. The Setter croft stands up the hill to the north east. Aim west from the loch up the South Lee of Setter and cross a ridged escarpment to a burn beside which is a stone enclosure. The next burn, at Haes Gu Dale, runs down past a large well constructed stone sheep pund and wash and into the sea. Ascend past a leaning standing stone to the summit of Brunt Hill and after a one and a half hour walk enjoy the view of Uyea Isle, Ronas Hill, North Roe, West Sandwick (Yell), Gloup (Yell), Saxa Vord (Unst) and the Ramna Stacks. Descend to a green tongue of land at Garmus Taing and follow the delightful stretch of coastline of Hevda. Enjoy high cliffs and sudden promontories at Tregeo and Viga where we cross the burn running down from Viga Water.

It is a bit of a haul round the Hill of Breibister but from it walk down into Fethaland and the neck of land connecting it to the Isle of

Fethaland. Here was once Shetland's busiest haaf fishing station. Today the ruins of over twenty fishing lodges stand silent round the shore. About 60 sixerns would have been stationed here between the beginning of June and the second week in August. Fish landed at Uyea, which had no suitable beach, were also taken to Fethaland for drying. Dominating the approach by sea from the north west stands a 5ft cairn; above the shingle beach on the south east side of the isthmus are the remains of two well-constructed stone boat noosts. Behind the noosts on the green plateau, between them and the stone wall, are the remains of a 'homestead'. The Inventory originally listed this mound as a 'broch (probable)' but admitted that there were no traces of any surrounding defensive works. Today all that is visible is the arc of a semi-circular wall and it is classified as an iron-age house site.

Ascend through the wall onto the 'isle' and keep to high ground near the precipitous west cliffs for sight of Burlee and most impressive Yellow Stack, near the lighthouse. Descend to the Point of Fethaland and after a three hour walk take a break and enjoy the view north over Stuack of the Ramna Stacks – once a bombing range and now an RSPB reserve. The northern extremity of the Point of Fethaland marks the harbour pilots' limit of the Port of Sullom Voe and tankers pick up and drop off pilots off this point.

Time now for us to turn south. The return along the east coast of the isle should include a study of a large rock face of steatite on the northern slope of Cleber Geo, where many generations of fishermen and others have carved names, hearts and dates. The oldest I have noticed is 1866. The Inventory notes that urns and bowls were cut out of the rock here, "the most extensive group of steatite workings in Shetland", and that, "exactly similar methods of working steatite were employed by the aborigines in many parts of North America".

Leave the Isle of Fethaland and head south east along the coast to Wick of Breibister and pass below the ruined croft of South House, the birthplace of photographer Jack Rattar (1876-

Charles Ratter.

1957) and the last inhabited house on Fethaland. Sadly Jack's father was drowned in the year of his birth but his Uncle Charles is remembered for being skipper of the last sixern, named the *Maggie*, to fish from Fethaland in the late 1890s. (see photograph above)

Jack Rattar (he changed his name from Ratter early in his professional career) became

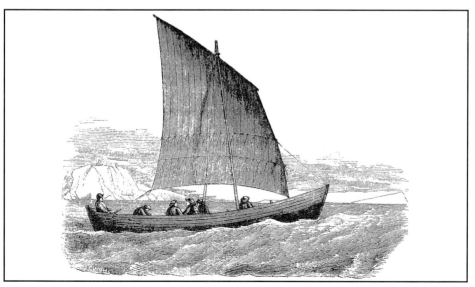

Shetland sixareen.

generally regarded as the best and best known of Shetland's early photographers. He was a pioneer of bird photography (and in 1926 a Shetland walrus). His pictures of Shetland landscapes can still "stir a longing in the hearts of the thousands of Shetlanders scattered all over the world, for in them love of their island home is intense".

Lanyar Taing protrudes north below the ruined croft and well preserved water mill of Skinisfield. Hibbert remarked that Fethaland is, "where grass is found to be so abundant and juicy that oxen feed theron both winter and summer", and there are many signs of ancient enclosures to be seen. The caves of Trumba attract sea birds, particularly kittiwakes. A large lump of quartz rock lies in the hill above the large sheep enclosure and very deep geo of Eislin Geo.

Climb up and over Ramna Beorgs and cross the plateau where Little Burn passes an ancient sheep cru. On Lokati Kame is an attractive natural arch below and the possible remains of a Celtic monastic site on top.

The building, rectilinear in structure, is similar to other known settlement ruins on the Kame of Isbister and Birrier, a site also to be viewed only from afar as access is now across a knife edge of rock.

Descend towards the valley leading to a beach below the Kame of Isbister. The Kame has been described by Dr K. O. Lamb as being the finest ancient coastal settlement site in the Northern Isles. The rock on which the settlement once stood is, "120ft high at the landward side and slopes 1 in 3 down towards the sea, giving a sloping grass-grown area, which is not visible from the land, of four-

Fethaland, by Jack Rattar.

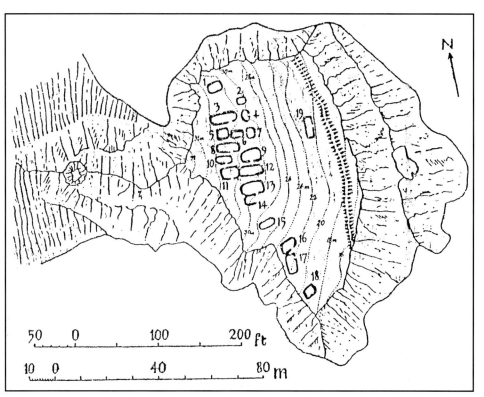

Kame of Isbister.

fifths of an acre. On the upper part of the slope are concentrated most of the 19 buildings now detectable". Twenty-three buildings were originally recorded here in the 1870s. Known locally as a 'Pictish graveyard', Dr Lamb considers this to be a monastic site possibly with Irish or Pict connections. Directly opposite on the west coast of Yell at Birrier is another similar site. It is not worth even attempting to cross over the kame; a view can be obtained of the slope from top of Head of Virdibrig (OS Virdibreck) – a climb well worth the effort.

There is then a gradual descent from the high cliffs to the Pund of Burravoe which is an enclosure north of the geo to which one descends. Climb up the eastern slopes of the Ward (which has a stone enclosure on its summit) and view the jagged Ravadale and Donald's Skerries. From the heights above the

Ness of Burravoe, The Neap and then the two small but colourful Holms of Burravoe, (known to fishermen as the 'Flooery Holms' due to the profusion of thrift covering them) complete with sheep, are visible. Cross a wire fence and descend to the promontory of Croo Green. There is a small natural arch at the north end and outcrops of soapstone on the beach.

Four earth mounds dominate the grazing area through which runs the remains of a turf wall. Two stones stand together near the mound at the south west corner, presumably all once part of a sheep fold.

Ascend the hill keeping a look-out for holes in the ground – the 'Graavin Hols' or 'Da Graavins' which are deep fissures sometimes disguised by undergrowth. At Burgo Taing all of North Roe is visible round Burra Voe. A sunken rock named The Flaess ('flat skerry') juts out in the middle of the entrance to this voe. The name of the voe indicates that a broch once guarded it but no trace of one survives. Traditionally, the site of it was near the point of the peninsula at Burgo Taing. Today, however, only two ruined crofts stand near rocky outcrops and look down on a derelict stone building.

This was once Davidson's fishing station of which the chimney has fallen and been reduced to six large blocks of rubble. Walk round the bay passing a small pund and four stone noosts before reaching a gate over which one reaches the pebble strand separating the sea from Loch of Beith. An ancient anchor protrudes from the pebbles. At Hou Banks stands North-Haa where John Williamson could once be seen skilfully preparing his internationally famous sheep-skin rugs.

Until 1929 the house served as a Hay & Co. store; the company also had interests in two fishing stations here. During the 1880s the new shop was built and "when herring curing began at North Roe the women were housed in a barn on the property hastily fitted with wooden beds and cooking facilities. In 1893 a wooden shed having two rooms", was erected "to provide accommodation for the beachmen in winter and spring and also for the women in summer", James Nicolson recounts.

Cross the pebble bar shielding the loch from the sea and join the main road. To the north stands the primary school on the left and on a knoll to the right the charming and well-proportioned church. There may be "a pub with no beer" in Australia – North Roe boasts a cemetery with no graves. The walled enclosure near the church, it was discovered on

John Williamson (John o' Lubba).

completion, enclosed ground which was unsuitable for the purpose intended.

Proceeding south on the road pass a fine memorial to those lost in the Great War, and the North Roe Methodist Church. This was established in 1828 and enlarged in 1858 following a visit by Rev. Samuel Dunn. On Sunday, 23rd January, 1825, he reported, "at 10, as no house could contain the people, I preached on a beach". Monday 24th "was prevented from going to Uyea by the storm. Preached from John 9.35 but never with such pain, the effects probably of speaking in the open air yesterday".

WALK 12: NORTH ROE – OLLABERRY ████████

12 miles (19 kms) : 6 hours

Cycle/Car: Car to Ollaberry, cycle to North Roe, 8 miles (13 km)

OS Maps: Explorer 469 Shetland Mainland – North West

A relaxing walk on low-level terrain presenting no great problems apart from some cliff fissures just before Loch End House comes into view, but plenty of interest. Good opportunity for bird-watching and wild life, particularly seals.

Leave North Roe by walking south along the main road until a modern pier is reached; here cross the shingle beach at The Wadill and with a big leap clear the burn. Cross a fence and follow the low banks of the Ness of Houlland eventually ascending slopes where in summer wild flowers create a riot of colour. The cliffs feature many inviting geos and the twin fingers of Wester and Easter Kame. Cross a fence and climb to Head of Calsta and look down on the rocks below, once used as places from which to fish in the sea ('craig-saets'). Descend to a plateau on which is the ruin of the croft of Calsta. The flare stack at Sullom Voe is visible.

The Bruiths of Calsta are long, black, jagged and ridged stretches of rock which the sea just separates from the mainland. Seals repose and snooze on them. 'The Castle' is the first of two rocks so named to be seen on this walk.

Cross the deep cleft of a burn and climb above Brei Geo, which has a grey shingly beach, to cross a fence and arrive at the ruined croft of Southton. Return to shore line, or stay high and follow an earth rampart which terminates at a fence. Descend past a stone ruin to Bio Geo which features a prominent stack and proceed round to a delightful settlement area dominated by the crofts at Skea, Northgardin, Newton and Midgardin, all connected by tracks to the main road.

Off The Knowes the promontory of Bu Taing heads east surrounded by the attendant skerries, Longa, Billia, Skea and Outer on which stands a black and white striped navigational aid. Grey seals occasionally haunt these skerries.

At Bu Taing is a stone ruin and there are boat noosts in the sandy bank. The next ruin may well have an advance guard of the flock of geese which patrols the rich pasture round Stourl, a croft which has electricity but not much sign of a road. Above South Hellia is a small ruin from which one climbs up and around Cleber Wick, which has a fine beach and cliffs containing soapstone. From here Colla Firth unfolds and the descent from the Height of Neap is made round Arvi Taing. Between the stout wire fence and the cliff edge are three dangerously deep fissures in the tussocky grass. One particularly long one is near the cliff edge; great care should be taken to avoid them. On a small plateau on the cliff edge is the grave of Robert Haldane. Today, all that is left of the enclosure (there was no head stone) are some very thin, rusty iron stakes and a small section of broken decorative railing. The impressive mansion of Lochend House has a hen house which, with its pointed window, resembles a miniature chapel. Originally, it was a window in the part of Lochend House dedicated for use as a chapel. Walk up to the fence at the rear of the house and follow it round until reaching a gate by a byre. Cross by the gate to pick up the cart track leading down round the walled garden to the shore. In 1902 Hay & Co. opened a shop at Lochend but in 1898 had sold the North Roe estate to Robert Camperdown Haldane who took up residence in Lochend House. He claimed descent from a Viking Danish King Halfdene and was a half brother of the politician Lord Haldane. Cross the loch's shingle bar, keeping clear of a tern colony in season and round the Ness of Housetter to Voe

Walk 12: NORTH ROE – OLLABERRY

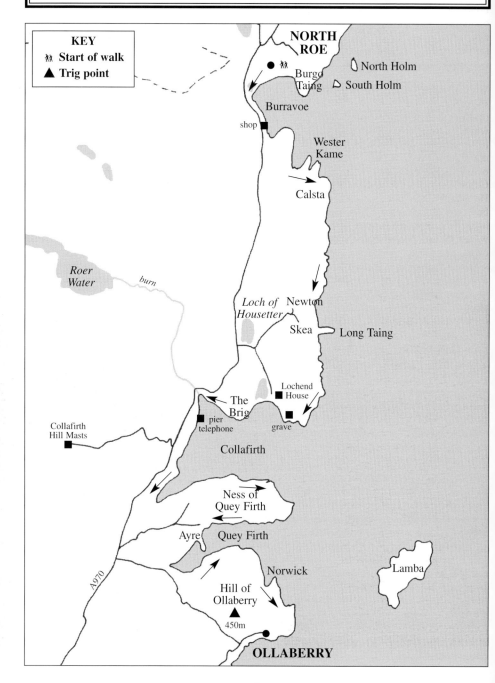

KEY
🚶 Start of walk
▲ Trig point

NORTH ROE

North Holm

Burgo Taing

South Holm

Burravoe

shop

Wester Kame

Calsta

Roer Water

burn

Loch of Housetter

Newton

Skea

Long Taing

Lochend House

The Brig

pier
telephone

grave

Collafirth Hill Masts

Collafirth

Ness of Quey Firth

Ayre

Quey Firth

A970

Norwick

Lamba

Hill of Ollaberry

▲
450m

OLLABERRY

of the Brig. Here Collafirth Pier was inaugurated in December 1988 and fishing boats may be seen tied up, sometimes offloading their catch. This is the latest development to a site on which sixty years ago stood a herring station, itself occupying the site of a former Norwegian whaling station.

Walk up to the main road and turn left past a sheep pund and wash. On the slopes of Beorgs of Housetter, just above the road north as it winds round over the bridge, 'The Brig', built in 1945 over the Burn of Roerwater, note masses of boulders. This feature, with two others locally, are part of the legend of the Collafirth Giant. Unlike Unst's Saxa and Herma, the Northmavine giant has no name but certainly has left his impression on the local landscape and legend. His main efforts were directed towards cattle rustling but as a civil engineer he was a failure. On the west slopes of the Beorgs of Housetter is the ruin of a stone enclosure. Marked 'Giants Garden' on OS, it is where the giant stored cattle and other items acquired by plunder. It is a very rocky area so providing material for his greatest project which was to extend the territorial range of his criminal activities by linking Collafirth to Yell by a causeway across Yell Sound. Unfortunately the nets holding the stones which he carried down to the sea were not strong enough and all the rocks fell out just before he got there. Subsequently the boulder strewn area was known as 'The Giant's Basket' or 'Maeshie' (a maeshie was a net constructed for carrying hay or corn on the back of a person or for attaching to a pony's pack-harness). Eventually the people rose up, attacked and captured the giant. Sentenced to death he was catapulted to his doom from an escarpment on top of the Beorgs.

After the bridge stay on the road, because the banks are small and contain peat cuttings, to pass stone enclosures and large sheep fold. The house Sundance has a magnificent plantation

Giant's grave.

61

of trees around it and there are more near the crofts of North and South Collafirth. Descend to cross over the Burn of Oxensetter to walk round Ness of Queyfirth. The many ruined crofts on its northern slope stand silently in contrast to the activity round the houses at the head of the voe.

Ruined noosts, jetties (one of which features a rusting chain) and other buildings, including one on the shore, will be seen. Climb up above many geos, some of which are sandy like Sandy Geo. On the east of the Ness the beach below The Ords is guarded by two rocks – another The Castle and Trolla Stack. The island of Lamba comes into view south east. Descend to Wottri where an electricity line terminates at a small lighthouse. Time now from North Roe about three hours.

Proceed up Quey Firth and descend to explore the ayre behind which is a splendid tidal basin, the Loch of Queyfirth, which never ebbs out. There are some stone ruins on the ayre and at the south end possibly a ruined, stone otter trap. Decide whether you are going to sensibly walk round the loch to a footbridge or, if the tide is out, splash through low water and climb onto the lower slopes of Hill of Ollaberry. At Hogan is a very large ruin of what must have

been a magnificent croft house and associated gardens and buildings. At Norwick is another croft ruin which looks down on to the beach. A large stone dyke, today backed by a modern fence with a metal gate, marks the frontier line to the hill area named Back of Ollaberry. Here a shallow depression, which crosses the end of the rounded headland from east to west, is the line of a geological fault. The depression can be followed down to the beach where it is exposed as dark, hard rock. A walk over the headland provides a superb route to end this walk. Climb up to the cliff line above Saberstone. At the hill's peak 62m (186ft) there is no mark but just below, on the west slope, is a small rectangular concrete slab. Descend, passing Pigeon Cove and Otter Had, where there are the remains of an old sheep pund, and enter the Bay of Ollaberry. The walled burial ground brings this walk to a grave conclusion; go to its right and follow the wall to a gate over which is the parking area at the west end of the church, which, fittingly for a township once named Olafsberg, is dedicated to St. Olaf.

Dr Cowie thought Ollaberry, "one of the prettiest spots in Shetland. On a fine summer evening nothing in the far north can excel the beauty of the scene".

Ollaberry kirk.

WALK 13: OLLABERRY – GLUSS AYRE ████████████████

8 miles (13 kms) : 4 hours

Cycle/Car: Car to Gluss Ayre, cycle to Ollaberry, 4 miles (7 km)

OS Maps: Explorer 469 Shetland Mainland – North West

The final stretch of the Round Northmavine Trek to Mavis Grind can be accomplished at quite a reasonable pace. It is possible to complete it via Gluss Isle in under seven hours and long distance walkers may prefer to do this. However this stretch conveniently breaks down into two sections and Walk 13 includes the 4 mile (7kms) walk round Gluss Isle. Gluss Ayre is reached by taking the A970 road north to Eela Water. Turn east onto the B9079 and leave it to take the unclassified road past Turvister, Nissetter, Bardister and Ramah to reach the road end for Waterside and Gluss Ayre.

After all the various challenges on the more rugged stretches of this coastline it feels strange to be able to pound along with no climbs apart from up The Neap. Most of the walk is on cliffside pasture land and there are many sheltered spots. Several crofts have been 'cleared' but enough remain to provide people with a lovely place to live and work whether in the main settlement areas at Ollaberry and Sullom or smaller but delightful Nissetter, Gluss and Haggrister.

Ollaberry Church is the place to commence this walk. In the church yard are memorials, ancient and modern, including decorated tombs at the east and west end and the War Memorial.

Cross the car park area, which includes a slip way. There is a post office and a telephone kiosk nearby. On the shore is a house named The Booth which is a reminder of Hanseatic League Merchant activities here in the 16th century and the small pier, complete with derrick, the main supply route in days gone by.

In 1789 the Gifford family built the magnificent Haa which stands four square and

well preserved. Admire it from the wall in the front of the walled garden where a path goes to a small shingle beach. Make for the main road to walk south from the village, most of which is overlooked by an outcrop on the slope of the hill above it known as The Berg, after which Olafsberg, now Ollaberry, was named. Follow the road past turnings to Leon and Kingland.

In the distance some way along the main road can be found the primary school, the community hall (a popular venue, particularly for summer Sunday teas) and the Ollaberry shop.

Turn left down the road signposted to East Ness and pass the redundant United Presbyterian Church and Manse which inspired John Reid's illustration in 1867.

The road passes above two sandy coves and passes over a sheltered burn where wildrose can grow in profusion. Make for the point of East Ness passing a large stone-lined boat noost above a shingle beach. On the Ness is a square stone ruin (a skeo?) from which one can enjoy a superb view of Ollaberry across the bay. Walk south along low banks below which a grey stack, The Kiln, stands 20ft high. Cross the deep cleft of a burn and a wire fence to climb on to the heathery slope of The Neap. Two masts on Gluss Isle come into view south. From the top of The Neap the jetties at Sullom Voe Terminal are visible.

Descend to cross a burn and shingle shore where stone boat noosts lie vacant and a track leads up to Fiblister.

At The Lother is a ruined croft – cross two fences and burn to reach and mount Skeo Knowe once known as 'Ola's Broch'. This is a prominent mound composed mainly of earth

Walk 13: OLLABERRY – GLUSS AYRE

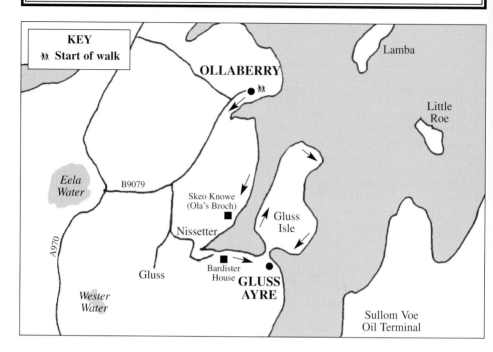

KEY
🚶 Start of walk

OLLABERRY

Lamba

Little Roe

Eela Water

B9079

Skeo Knowe (Ola's Broch)

Gluss Isle

Nissetter

A970

Gluss

Bardister House

GLUSS AYRE

Wester Water

Sullom Voe Oil Terminal

Ola's broch.

and small granite stones or chips on the edge of the bank that overlooks the beach, approximately 12ft high. Not a broch, it is probably a natural formation which the Inventory describes as a burial-place in prehistoric times. A cinerary urn of steatite clay of the Bronze Age type was found here and is now in the National Museum. There are no signs of a cist but the mound has been cut in two places, one cavity on the top and one on the side nearest the sea.

Near the croft of Nissetter, at HU 356778, an underground house was discovered in 1900 by the crofter, whilst ploughing. The plough disturbed lintel stones of a chamber, thought to be a souterrain, at about 6ins below ground surface. It contained a fireplace and at least two steatite vessels, since destroyed. There is now no trace of this underground structure.

All round the area wild flowers blazing gold, red and yellow, grow dense in summer. Walk the shingle shore to a ruined croft, cross the burn and climb 100 yards onto the road. Follow the road east, OS marked 'Boat House', where the noble Bardister Haa awaits full restoration. The boat house was where supplies were originally landed and beside it once stood a shop. The Haa is not OS marked but is another Shetland historic house which has fortunately survived.

At Gluss Ayre the house, Waterside, has been restored and faces across the entrance of Sullom Voe towards the storage tanks of the terminal. Decision time: to walk the four miles round Gluss Isle and add an hour to the walk, or not?

If yes, then cross the ayre, pass through a gate and follow the track to Mast 1. From there stay high and head north along a green path through heather and peat banks to Mast 2.

It could now be three hours since you left Ollaberry but standing above Ingli Geo opposite The Kiln one feels almost back where one began. There are compensations – particularly the views north and north east of Yell. At the eastern corner is an 8ft high wooden V marker where one can enjoy a final look north before aiming south once more.

There may be no sign of human habitation on Gluss Isle but the presence of seals in Yarfils Wick will cheer one up.

The seals can be so tame here they almost clamber onto the shingle beach to make better aquaintance once disturbed from their resting places on the low, red crags. Pass another V sign and at Tivaka Taing there is a concrete installation which houses a 352 metre boom. This can be deployed to a yellow buoy – one of eight boomsites which are part of the Sullom Voe Terminal's pollution response capability. Return to the ayre via a sheepfold.

WALK 14: GLUSS AYRE – MAVIS GRIND ▰▰▰▰▰

9 miles (15 kms) : 4 hours

Cycle/Car: Car to Mavis Grind, cycle to Gluss Ayre, 9 miles (15 km)

OS Maps: Explorer 469 Shetland Mainland – North West

It is fittingly easy walking for the final stretch of the Northmavine Trek but there is much to savour. We are on the quiet side of Sullom Voe where crofting remains the main occupation but the possibilities of quarrying are occasionally raised.

From Gluss Ayre head south to round the Ness of Bardister. A small lighthouse, fed by an overhead electric cable, comes into view and the Loch of Scadafleek is a tern colony. Otters may be spotted in Dale Voe – they use Dale Burn and have holts between this loch and Maggie Kettle's loch and ayre further south. Many years ago, according to folk lore, a certain Maggie crossed from Delting in a kettle and landed here, her 'ship' being the first iron vessel to navigate Sullom Voe. What would

Walk 14: GLUSS AYRE – MAVIS GRIND

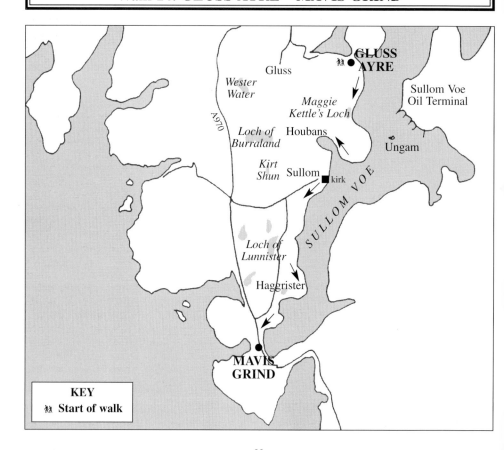

KEY

🚶 Start of walk

Maggie's kettle.

she make of the thousands of oil tanker movements which have taken place here since 1978?

There are more seals to be seen at Noust of Burraland; they may have become bored with lying up on the rock Ungam which sticks out in the widest part of Sullom Voe (nearly 2 miles across). Most of Sullom Voe Terminal is visible from here. To the right of the four jetties is the process area whilst on the hill of Vats Houlland stand the crude oil storage tanks.

Millions of barrels of oil have been processed by the terminal since it began operations in November 1978. Construction cost £1.2 billion and involved over 7000 construction workers who built Europe's largest oil terminal to a design which sought to minimise its impact on the environment. Today production is now less than one million barrels of oil a day, but the revenue generated by the oil and gas exported from here continues to make a massive contribution to the local and national economy.

It was not the first major cause of disruption to the quiet of the voe. In 1939 the Royal Air Force established an airfield at Scatsta and the waters of Sullom Voe became a base for RAF Coastal Command and Royal Norwegian Air Force flying boats, mainly Catalinas and Sunderlands. A VC was awarded to Flt Lt Cruikshank stationed here in July 1944 and many other brave flights were made by the so called 'Arctic Airmen' who flew to Russia and attempted to reach the North Pole. "We rounded the valley's end," wrote an RAF Intelligence Officer, Derek Gilpin Barnes, stationed here in the war, "to see the first change of landscape since dawn – the sullen waters of Sullom Voe, ablink with the riding lights of aircraft at their moorings. In the camouflaged huts, huddled on that desolate shore, were many young men all dreaming of trams and girls, fish bars, pictures, 'the dogs' and 'home', and all shouting or singing or turning on radios – to drown the thin, insistent voices of an earlier age."

Sullom Voe has meant many things to both airmen and oilmen. Its name 'Sullom' derives from the old Norwegian word 'sotheimr' and means 'a place in the Sun' which has caused many a wry smile.

All are aware of the transitory nature of their presence. Gilpin Barnes again: "The moment we packup and go, these low hills will shrug their dark shoulders and settle back into the slumber of the centuries. These chill northern airs will put a touch of rust and decay upon all we leave behind – and resume their uninterrupted silences."

At Fugla Ayre on the south east corner of the Ness is another boom site and most of Sullom Voe, Shetland's largest voe, comes into view. The Long Ayre near the entrance to The Houb, which is protected by a chevron shaped boom, might tempt one to take a short cut. Don't! The electricity poles may stride straight across but better for us to enjoy the walk round the shingle shore in front of the delightful sheltered house of Houbans. Here are bushes in profusion and a bridge crosses Seali Burn to join a maintained track which leads south to Askelon. This is the first of four houses which were given Biblical place names in Sullom, the others being Gaza, Ekron and Gath (but no Sodom, one has to walk Whalsay to find that!). Follow the road to the track down to the well maintained church, built in 1865 but ready to face another century at least with new windows and door. The Manse stands alongside but the cemetery is another five minutes walk south. Within the walled enclosure are memorials to Sullom folk and others including Able Seaman Frederick Taylor, HMS *Isis*, who is commemorated by both an official Navy headstone and the original wooden cross created locally. Along the south wall another memorial commemorates Samuel Neil, "Author, Teacher and Shakespearian Scholar".

There are deserted crofts in the hill and a modern jetty on the foreshore near Gaza. A plantation of trees catches the eye and in summer the fields are full of cottongrass. A horseshoe shape of boulders stands by a ruined concrete building at Marki Ness. At the Houb of Lunnister look up the delightful dale to see the tumbling burn passing a ruined watermill 200 yards up stream. So onto Ness of Haggrister where a spit of land offers another, softer lie-up place for the seals. Everybody here has a view south of the village of Brae. Turn into the Bight of Haggrister and cross the red shingle bar which keeps the sea from the loch. It is a well-sheltered spot which has encouraged the establishment of two plantations of trees – clumps of wildrose bushes screen the fence and protect the saplings. There are ancient noosts cut into the banks and long dilapidated hulks of fishing boats which one passes before climbing up to a fence.

Mavis Grind finally comes into view from a turf/stone enclosure on South Ness; a low stone building stands on the shore edge in front of which a large noost has been cut into the bank. Climb up towards the croft, noting two ruined planticrubs, and stay high to follow a sheep trail until Skipadock is reached. This is a white house near the road down onto which one looks after one has rounded the hill and its name means 'Safe Haven'. You may think this entirely appropriate as you finally descend to the main road and follow it south to where the Round Northmavine Trek all began – Mavis Grind.

Who would have thought that so narrow a gate could have opened up into an area so large and so rich in natural and historical treasure?

CIRCULAR WALK A

MANGASTER – LANG HEAD – MANGASTER

6 miles (10 kms) : 3 hours

OS Maps: Explorer 469 Shetland Mainland – North West

A walk to the coast via Punds Water, where there are two remarkable Neolithic ruins, and back along the dramatic coastline and the shore of Mangaster Voe.

Drive to the junction of the A970 and road down to Mangaster. Walk up the hill in a westerly direction, descending over a ridge just before the loch of Punds Water is reached. On a plateau above the south shore a mound of stones will be seen which closer inspection will reveal to be the best surviving heel-shaped cairn on Mainland Shetland (see aerial colour photograph). It is estimated to have a 50ft facade, the outer ends of which are prolonged

into horns. At the centre of the facade a roofless entrance leads to a roofless, trefoil shaped, cairn chamber 6ft square. Built of white granite boulders, measuring on average about 2ft by 1ft, it rises some 5ft above the surface of the knoll on which it stands. The walls of the chamber, which still stand 4ft 9 inches high, are built in regular courses of masonry without any use of upright slabs. The floor is not paved but covered with clay which has red water-rolled pebbles embedded in it. The roof of the cairn has collapsed inwards.

Descend to Punds Water and walk round to the promontory which thrusts into the loch at the

Punds Water from the air. Heel-shaped cairn in foreground. Neolithic homestead in background.

69

Circular Walk A: MANGASTER – LANG HEAD – MANGASTER

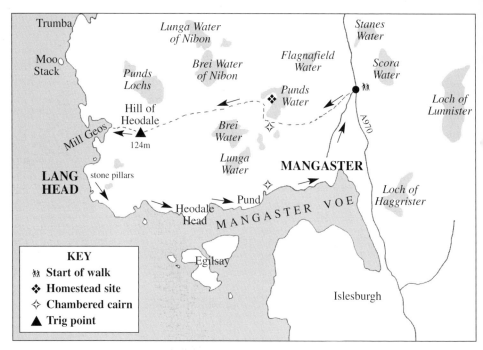

KEY
- 🏃 Start of walk
- ❖ Homestead site
- ◇ Chambered cairn
- ▲ Trig point

Punds Water chambered cairn.

start of which is another chambered cairn or possibly Neolithic homestead ruin (OS marked 'homestead'). Five compartments and a paved entrance passage remain of this notable structure which had an external diameter of approximately 33ft.

Walk west keeping to the north of Brei Water and climb up to the Hill of Heodale (spot height 124m) which provides a superb vantage point for viewing the area. Descend to Mill Geos with its dramatic stacks and natural arches and walk south to Lang Head where there is a noble cairn.

From here follow the coastline south round Stivva, the Black Skerry of Ramago and into North Sound where the islands of Egilsay are divided inequally by a deep cliff. Heodale Head had a medieval chapel site; there is a pund on the cliff edge, could this be it? Cross Heo Dale to reach the Pund of Mangaster where there is a house but no road. From here

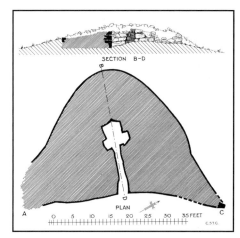

Punds Water chambered cairn plan.

descend to cross the deep chasm of Gill Burn which flows into Mangaster Voe. From here make for the road end at Mangaster and so back to the A970.

CIRCULAR WALK B ███████████████████

NIBON

4 miles (6 kms) : 2 hours – A 'there and back' walk. For additional information see Walk 3

OS Maps: **Explorer 469 Shetland Mainland – North West**

This is a pleasant stroll which starts from Gunnister at the end of an unclassified road which heads north west from the A970 shortly after the road to Sullom at Johnnie Mann's loch. One has the option of walking the quiet unclassified road which branches off west to Nibon shortly before Gunnister is reached or sometimes walking the banks near the road.

It was at Gunnister that in May 1951 the remains of the 'The Gunnister Man' were found in a shallow grave. His purse contained some silk ribbon and three late seventeenth century coins of low value. Nobody knows who he was but his clothes are on display in the Royal Scottish Museum, Edinburgh.

Follow the south shore of Gunnister Voe and note the Isle of Gunnister across North Sound and the Isle of Nibon with its natural arch, opposite Nibon across South Sound. Nibon is a most attractive spot and although only the Captain's House, built as a home for Captain Bigland, is a permanent home, there is a self-catering accommodation available. Keep a lookout for otters as you explore the surrounding areas of sea-shore and cliff.

On the return to Gunnister note the many abandoned dwellings and signs of extensive crofting activities in this area in the past.

Circular Walk B: NIBON

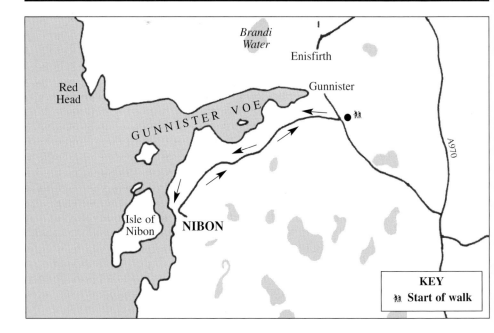

KEY
🚶 Start of walk

72

One walker who came to grief – 'The Gunnister Man'.

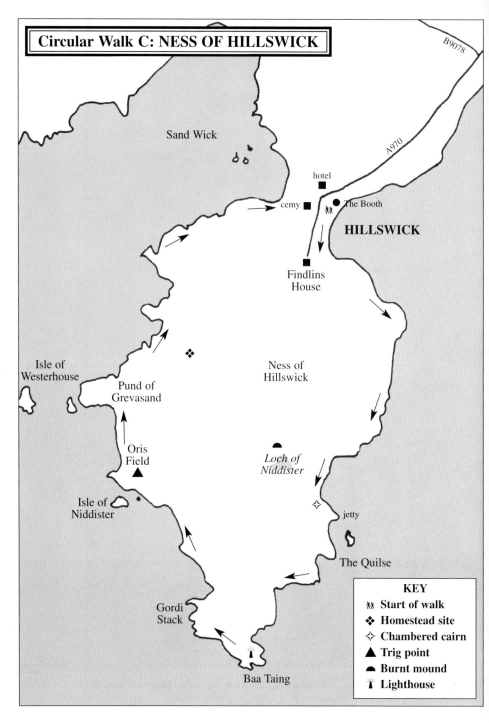

Circular Walk C: NESS OF HILLSWICK

B9078

A970

Sand Wick

hotel

cemy   The Booth

HILLSWICK

Findlins
House

Isle of
Westerhouse

Ness of
Hillswick

Pund of
Grevasand

Oris
Field

*Loch of
Niddister*

Isle of
Niddister

jetty

The Quilse

Gordi
Stack

Baa Taing

KEY

ᛮᛮ **Start of walk**
❖ **Homestead site**
✧ **Chambered cairn**
▲ **Trig point**
◖ **Burnt mound**
ⵎ **Lighthouse**

NESS OF HILLSWICK

5 miles (8 kms) : 3 hours

OS Maps: **Explorer 469 Shetland Mainland – North West**

This splendid walk starts at The Booth in Hillswick, now the Da Bod Café. It follows the coastline in a clockwise direction. It is a classic Shetland walk and not to be missed. Good otter spotting country.

We should aim south east for the Ness, proceeding round the 10ft high garden wall of The Booth and looking into the old walled burial ground. This was established on the site of the medieval chapel site dedicated to St. Gregory. In 1733 another church was built a short distance away to be replaced by the present St. Magnus. On entering the burial

ground metal gate two decorated memorial stones will be found built into the wall on the right and one on the left. Both date post 1707.

In 1870, in a kitchen midden near this site, were found four long-handled bone weaving combs (now in the National Museum) and remains of roe and red deer dating from the Iron Age.

The big house on the left with red granite blocks in its garden walls is The Manse. Above it are Findlins House and on the right, complete with horses and carts, is The Smithy

Hillswick burial ground memorials.

Cairn at Bight of Niddister.

and behind it Findlins Farm. The nearby bay is a good place to spot an otter. The terrain is usually quite marshy and it only improves after a fence has been crossed and a little height gained. At Tur Ness the sea has bored a hole through the cliff to create a rock pool and there is a larger version a little further on at the end of a row of boulders marking a sheep pund.

At Leadie is a large stone enclosure and a sheep wash; a little further on is a small stone ruin with a small double cave in the cliff below.

Where the burn runs down from the loch to the Bight of Niddister are the remains of a water mill and small stone ruin. Follow the burn 300yds onto the plain and on a point of a low promontory at the west end of the Loch of Niddister is a crescentic burnt mound measuring 17m long, 14m broad and 1.7m high with two boulders on its north west slope. Apart from their uses in cooking and sauna

bathing, it has also been suggested that they may have been used in early woollen textile production, which requires heat and moisture for the fulling process. Fulling is the means of cleansing, shrinking and thickening cloth. Considering how many sheep have been farmed in Shetland, a link to cloth processing with some burnt mounds is not improbable. Our ancestors needed clothes here as anywhere else and also, presumably, laundering facilities.

The remains of a prehistoric cairn are visible at HU 280755. Severely mutilated it stands on a low ridge about 50ft above the sea at the Bight of Niddister. Within the cairn are two blocks and some slabs suggesting the remains of a chamber.

At the next burn, down the cliff by a stone ruin, run some steps to a jetty, once used by boats servicing the lighthouse. Commence the climb above a natural arch and quaintly named The

The Drongs.

Quilse islet. It's a bit of a haul above the sweep of Queen Geos. Descend along the magnificent cliff battlements – The Drongs come into view for the first time – and approach the lighthouse on Baa Taing by following a regimented black and white column of fence posts. The lighthouse marks the entrance to Ura Firth and many a ship must have been glad to leave the turbulent waters of St. Magnus Bay by passing it, the winking light well to port.

The west coastline of the Ness of Hillswick is most dramatic. The massive Gordi Stack, which Tudor thought, "from one point of view represents a rhinoceros horn", can be appreciated from three vantage points, with the 'rhino view' being the middle one.

The cliffs are precipitous and great care is needed on leaving a view of the stack as one is walking up a deceptive slope of the hill, unaware of the long drop awaiting the unwary. Descend to pass over a stone wall with boulders, set like Fetlar's famous Finniegirt, and climb to the spot height of Oris Field. This is on a knoll, the stones of which show traces of whitewash and two theodolite holes. Descend to the Pund of Grevasand where there is an excellent view of Isle of Westerhouse and

Gordi Stack with the Drongs in the background.

Pund of Grevasand Neolithic settlement.

The Drongs – in a heavy sea the water slices through its arches with such fury one is amazed the feature has survived for so long. One can walk out along the pund by stepping over a stone wall but keep down on the northern slope and be warned – this peninsula also comes to an abrupt end!

If one now turns round and heads east up onto the highest hill behind, there is a granite pyramid on the flat area on top – is this the 'red unhewn obelisk of granite, mantled with grey moss, being the memorial of far remote times',

Granite obelisk.

that Hibbert waxed lyrical about? It's not particularly red.

Pass a cairn of stones and descend to the OS 'homestead'. This is the ruin of a Neolithic oval house, field boundaries and clearance cairns of what was an Early Bronze Age settlement area. This example, about 60ft outside circumference, has a low oval stone and turf wall surrounding a hollow centre. There is clear evidence of the entrance on the east side.

In the valley below to the north a burn runs down to the cliffs. Descend to a fence and climb to the spot height (82m), the highest point of the Ness. There are the remains of four metal stays in the concrete. Descend again, to Ber Dale and make the most of the remainder of the coastline before passing a large stone clearance cairn, piles of boulders and coming to a wall.

Follow the cliff walk outside the fence and drop down on to the pebbly beach, once particularly valued as a place for drying fish. Cross the pebbly field behind it to a gate and one is back outside The Booth once more.

CIRCULAR WALK D

ESHANESS LIGHTHOUSE – STENNESS

4 miles (6 kms) : 2 hours

OS Maps: **Explorer 469 Shetland Mainland – North West**

Stenness, by John Reid (1869).

A walk round one of Shetland's most well known stretches of coastline, returning to Stenness by road in order to visit Cross Kirk, the broch on Sae Brei and the burnt mound at Loch of Breckon. For further information see Walk 6.

Start this walk from the beach at Stenness. Cross a wire fence and follow the low cliffs past a stone ruin and a planticrub. Seals frequent this area and there are small natural arches to be seen.

Cross another wire fence and dilapidated stone wall to reach a shingle beach into which a burn flows from the Loch of Breckon. There were originally two water mills here; the lower one has virtually gone but the upper mill is an excellent ruin. Across on the Isle of Stenness, kittiwakes nest on North Stole. On The Bruddans seals bask. Ascend the pebble strewn slopes past a ruined crub and decide whether to obtain a closer view of The Cannon blow hole. It involves climbing over some very slippy rocks but in the right conditions the sound and sight of it are memorable – the sea is forced out

of the cave, "with a loud noise and a copious discharge of fine foam not unlike the report and smoke of a piece of ordnance", enthused Cowie.

From here follow the burn up to a dam of large boulders on the shore of Gerdie Loch. At the Wend there is a mound of stones on a spit of land. Follow the southern shore and climb the hill Sae Breck to see its trig point (61m), a

Cross near Stenness, with Dore Holm in the background.

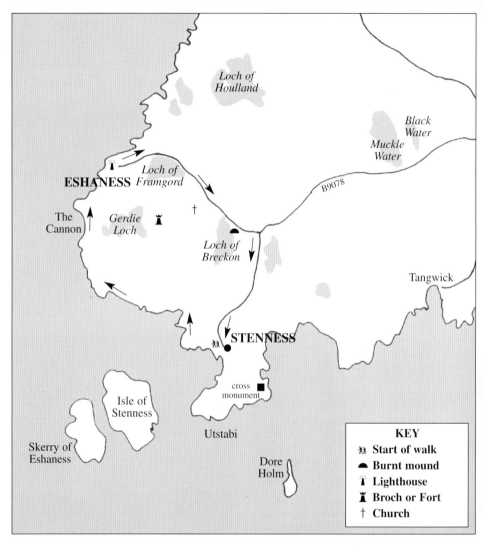

Loch of
Houlland

Black
Water

Muckle
Water

ESHANESS *Loch of Framgord*

B9078

The
Cannon

*Gerdie
Loch*

†

Loch of
Breckon

Tangwick

STENNESS

cross
monument

Isle of
Stenness

Utstabi

Skerry of
Eshaness

Dore
Holm

KEY
🚶 **Start of walk**
▲ **Burnt mound**
⚲ **Lighthouse**
⚔ **Broch or Fort**
† **Church**

disused coastguard hut and some derelict World War II defence installations complete with blast walls. The views from here are superb and the ditches of the prehistoric fort remain to remind one of the role Sae Breck has filled throughout history as a defended look-out. This is a broch site and there remains a central mound and enclosing ditch. Around it is a circular earthen bank with a diameter of 112ft from crest to crest. Nowhere more than 2ft high it is thought the bank was once much higher because the debris extends over a 16ft width.

Below, north west, is the site of the medieval Cross Kirk, some sections of its wall still

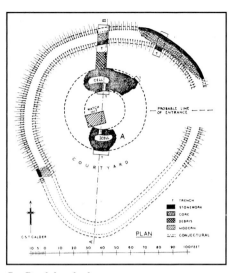

Sae Breck broch plan.

standing nearly 4ft high in the Eshaness burial ground. It was dedicated to the Holy Rood and was traditionally one of the principal chapels of pilgrimage in Shetland.

Cowie describes how the snails living in the derelict kirk walls were "collected, dried, powdered and prescribed as a remedy for jaundice". And on Candlemas (2nd February) it was customary to walk to the chapel ruin at dead of night with lighted candles, which were duly solemnized and kept to be lit at future times, "whenever thunder was heard or the malevolence of demons was apprehended". This tradition so upset a minister of Northmavine, it is said that he arranged for the old kirk to be destroyed.

One memorial of certain notoriety will be found on the right hand side of the entrance path in front of a seventeenth century 5ft long heraldic memorial. A transcript of the lettering on the tomb is printed on a display board and reads: "Donald Robertson, born 4 January 1783. Died 4 June 1842. Aged 63 years. He was a peaceable quiet man, and, to all appearance, a sincere Christian; his death was much regretted, which was caused by the stupidity of Laurance Tulloch in Clothister who sold him nitre instead of Epsom Salts, by

which he was killed in the space of 3 hours after taking a dose of it." Damned from here to eternity! Tulloch, no doubt much to local relief, moved from the district and opened a shop in Aberdeen in 1852. A memorial stone to 'Johnnie Notions' Williamson has been placed on a slab indicating his grave and in the top left-hand corner of the burial ground there is a memorial bench which incorporates a violin in its design. It commemorates the 20th anniversary of Shetland's Young Heritage and its founder Doctor Tom Anderson MBE, who is buried in lair 23 next to the bench.

The church was originally oblong in plan and measured 34ft 10ins from east to west by 20ft 3ins from north to south. The only opening traceable is the entrance centred in the west gable. A 17th century tomb slab with an illegible Latin text survives in the burial ground and a small bronze figurine of a horse found here has been identified as a 14th century Scandinavian scale-weight.

Below the burial ground on the shore line of Loch of Breckon at its north east end is a crescentic burnt mound, 18m x 10m x 1.2m. Two helpful stiles allow one to enjoy a walk to it and round the loch.

Leave this loch to cross back over Sae Breck and return to the cliffs beyond The Cannon. The Eshaness lighthouse dominates the view;

Bronze horse – a 14th century depiction of a Shetland pony?

this stands 200ft above the sea and was built in 1929. The cliffs named The Slettans are high level, wave-cut rocks formed in an extinct volcano and opposite the south end of the lighthouse is the Kirn (Churn) O'Slettans, a deep narrow funnel with the sea boiling at its base. In stormy weather the sea has been known to shoot up the funnel and over the lighthouse. It would be a dangerous place to slip. Behind the lighthouse is a car park area and an excellent illustrated information display board on natural and historical features of Eshaness.

From here walk down the road to where it joins the B9078 to walk south visiting, in turn, the kirk, broch and a burnt mound. The road ends back at Stenness.

CIRCULAR WALK E

ESHANESS LIGHTHOUSE – HAMNAVOE – ESHANESS LIGHTHOUSE

5 miles (8 kms) : 3 hours

OS Maps: Explorer 469 Shetland Mainland – North West

Another well known and remarkable stretch of coastline which includes dramatic cliff scenery, a broch site, the Hole of Scraada, Grind of the Navir and Hamna Voe. For more information see Walk 6.

From the road end at Esha Ness lighthouse walk north and proceed past some large boulders round South Head of Caldersgeo, another car park area with redundant Royal Navy notice board, and admire Calder's Geo – it is very deep. A subterranean passage connects the north side with the open sea. There are kittiwakes and fulmars in the next geo which is reached by ascending to a wall and climbing over a stile. Pass the Lochs of Dridgeo and view the massive Moo Stack, noting a leg shaped natural arch at its north end. Shortly after this, look east and when the mound of a broch is visible on the shore line of the Loch of Houlland, turn inland and walk towards it. Keep a sharp look-out for the Hole of Scraada; this is a long opening in the ground 132 yards from end to end and narrow all the way. At the base of its cliffs is a beach into which the sea flows through a subterranean passage 110 yards long. Originally there were two 'Holes' but on 9th October, 1873 a natural bridge separating the two collapsed into the void beneath, shortly after Morgan Thomason had crossed it on horseback. The burn from the Loch of Houlland bubbles down into the eastern end of the Hole with sufficient energy to have once powered three water mills.

The view of the mills is enhanced by the backdrop of cascading water and the broch which dominates a small promontory which juts out from the north west into the loch. It is an impressive ruin with walls on the north and north east surviving to a height of 12ft. Overall diameter is 57ft and the wall is 15ft thick. The

entrance, which is at the west south west is 3ft wide at the mouth. On the right is the traditional cell or guard chamber.

Three lines of defence can be seen with an entrance passage 5ft wide running through the two outer lines and over the inner bank. At the south end of the headland the broch was connected to the adjacent island by a causeway

Gale at Eshaness.

Circular Walk E: ESHANESS LIGHTHOUSE – HAMNAVOE – ESHANESS LIGHTHOUSE

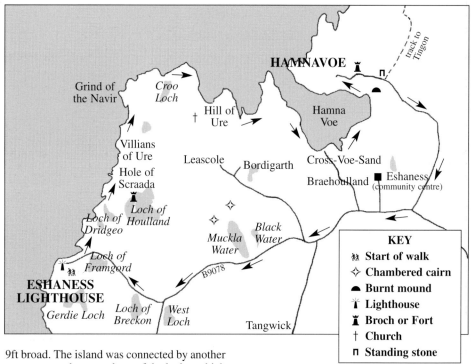

KEY

🏃 Start of walk
✧ Chambered cairn
● Burnt mound
Ⓧ Lighthouse
Ⓧ Broch or Fort
† Church
∏ Standing stone

9ft broad. The island was connected by another causeway to the west shore of the loch – which presumably helps the sheep to graze the island.

Around the broch the sub-rectangular and oval foundation ruins of a later, possibly Pictish, settlement, have been identified.

Further inland between the Loch of Houlland and Muckla Water the OS marks two chambered cairns. The more westerly one is the March Cairn, Hamars of Houlland, which stands 5ft 6 inches high and measures 33ft 6ins from north west to south east and 34ft 6ins from north east to south west. This cairn, a square example of a heel-shaped type, is a puzzle to the archaeologists because, against the general pattern, its chamber was entered by a passage which opened from the eastern side, and this side did not have a facade. (see plan page 34)

Return to the cliffs at Scraada and cross stiles over the wire fences to reach the fertile plateau named the Villians of Ure. The green turf stretches for over a mile along the coast and about half a mile inland.

The cliffs abound in caves and natural arches, the rocks ceaselessly scarred by the violence of the waves. One prominent stack, 200ft offshore and about 300ft high, is the Maiden Stack. After passing Gruna Stack comes the Grind of the Navir ('gate of the borer'), a natural feature which has attracted attention above all other on Eshaness.

The Atlantic has found a weak spot in the cliff face and smashed through it leaving the vertical sides of the breach open to view and smoothed by the action of the waves. The

84

breach is 36ft wide with a lower step 40ft above the sea. The sides are 45ft in height. Behind it is a basin of about 90ft in diameter filled with water. Huge cubical blocks of rock rise from the edge of the basin; the blocks have been torn from the cliffs and driven back into the breach. It is possible to descend through the gateway to view the sea between the high rock walls.

Red rocks predominate whether on the Head of Stanshi or in the large dilapidated walls of the sheep pens on the cliffs nearby. At the point and stack of The Burr is a boulder-strewn foreshore between the sea and Croo Loch; a small roofless building sits on the loch's west shore and beside the burn flowing into its south end is a ruined water mill. Ascend the slopes of the Hill of Ure to view Shalder Sound and many seals basking on the reef of rocks named the Targies. Away out to sea north the natural arch through the offshore island of Muckle Ossa is visible. On the Hill of Ure at North House is a medieval chapel site and burial ground. The chapel building was traditionally associated with a croft out-building situated on a small knoll but 'kirkure' has long since disappeared.

There are burns to be crossed at the Geo and the boggy Dale of Ure on the slopes of which stands a solitary crub in the shape of a 4ft high tower. Descend to the headland of Raasmi where there are seven stone enclosures of various shapes and sizes.

We are now entering Hamna Voe, another notable fishing station in the past and a salmon cage maintains a tradition today. From a marshy area a burn flows to the foreshore with two crubs by it. Upstream is a derelict water mill with two surviving mill stones. Other signs of past activity are an abandoned croft, four more planticrubs and three ruined stone fishing lodges on the cliff edge. Follow a fence down past a derelict Haa, with two standing stones in its garden, and a croft, before crossing the sandy beach of Cross-voe-sand. Over the road leading to the salmon farm jetty is a stile to help one on the way to Hoohivda. Beside this croft a fast flowing burn runs under a well constructed footbridge and artist Paul Whitworth has established a studio gallery here.

From Hamnavoe follow the road south past the broch site (notable for its ditches) and the two standing stones, the Giant's Stones. Join the A9708 at Braewick and return to Eshaness lighthouse visiting the Neolithic homestead site near Black Water and the chambered cairns at Muckla Water as time allows.

CIRCULAR WALK F

HAMNAVOE – TINGON – HAMNAVOE

5 miles (8 kms) : 3 hours

OS Maps: **Explorer 469 Shetland Mainland – North West**

Memorable coastal walking combined with a stroll through the countryside, with a broch site and prehistoric standing stones for added interest. For further information see Walk 7.

Leave 'Johnnie Notion's house' at Hamnavoe and walk west down to the cliffs of Riva Taing; the land has been cultivated and there are occasional gatherings of boulders. Cross a

Circular Walk F: HAMNAVOE – TINGON – HAMNAVOE

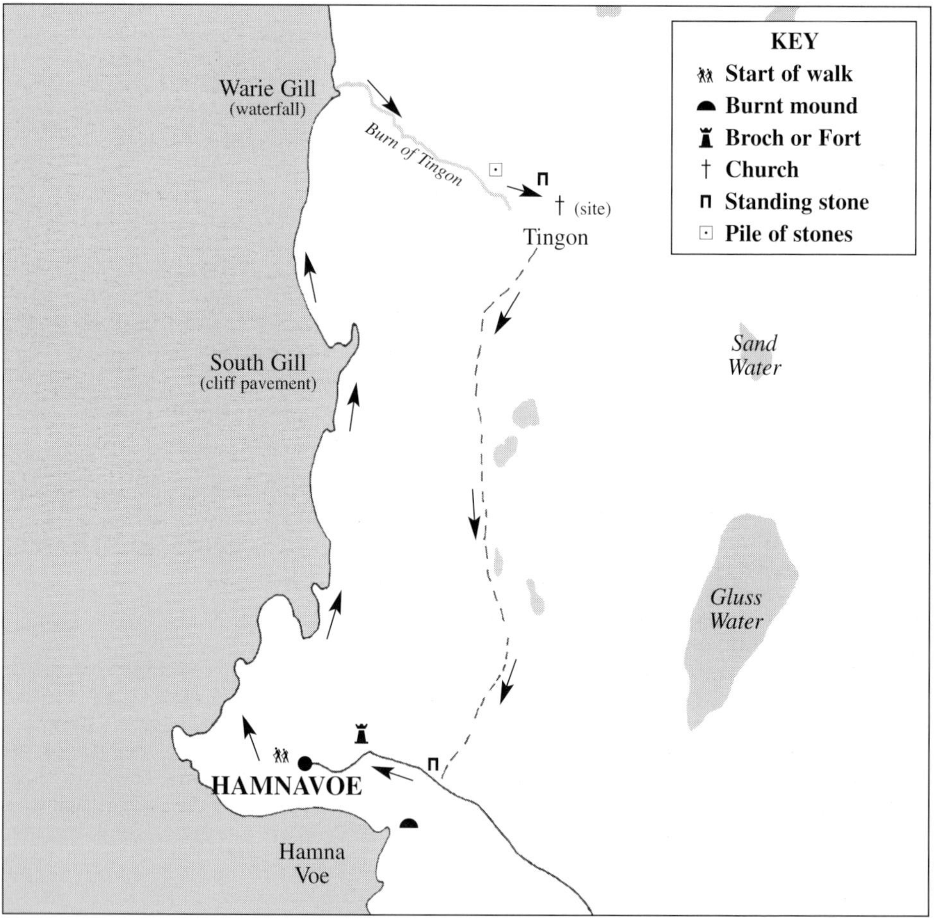

KEY
Start of walk
Burnt mound
Broch or Fort
Church
Standing stone
Pile of stones
Warie Gill
(waterfall)
Burn of Tingon
(site)
Tingon
South Gill
(cliff pavement)
Sand Water
Gluss Water
HAMNAVOE
Hamna Voe

fence to reach the boulder beach of Whal Wick where there is a view up the burn towards the broch. Cross another fence and cross a marshy boulder-strewn area with large dilapidated stone enclosures and sheep wash. Some large stones lie together resembling collapsed dolmens. The small stone ruin spotted 400yds into the hill is not a mill though there are mill lochs above. From Hoken one is on the Villains of Hamnavoe, walking is easy going. Pass a tarn, low stone wall and another tarn. At South Gill the cliff height increases and includes black rock shelving. The burn from Punds Water cascades over the cliff.

Cross a high stone wall to ascend to Erne's House, a 4ft cairn standing on a stone pavement. There is a small tarn behind the cairn and on a hillock east of the tarn are stones set in the shape of a cist.

At the north side of Warie Gill view two huge caves in the base of the sheer, black cliff. The eroded lava cliffs sometimes have peculiar shapes, and a lump of lava resembling the head of a camel stares defiantly out to sea. It is here, where the Burn of Tingon flows down to the sea, that we turn inland and follow the burn to the track heading south from Tingon. Tingon is the site of a medieval chapel but the walls of the building associated with it have completely tumbled. The wall dimensions measure 9 metres east-west and 3.5 metres north-south. To investigate the 'Pile of Stones' shown on the OS map follow the Burn of Tingon to where the concrete footbridge incorporating a bedstead and bottles has sadly collapsed, but still affords a route to cross. On the slope of a hill over a fence is a striking standing stone, roughly measuring 5ft high, 8ft circumference and 2ft broad. It is angled slightly towards the west. The 'Pile of Stones' is just that and beyond it is the ruin of a large croft.

The large house, named Newton, still stands at Tingon and was once lived in by landowners who made their fortunes in the Australian goldmines and returned home to buy land in this area and evict the local crofters.

Standing stone at Tingon.

Turn south along the track until it reaches the main road. At the junction stand the two Giant's Stones standing stones. Turn west along the road to return to Hamnavoe, the broch site with its impressive ditches is on the right of the road before the main settlement is reached.

CIRCULAR WALK G ▬▬▬▬▬▬▬▬▬▬

HEYLOR

6 miles (10 kms) : 3 hours

OS Maps: **Explorer 469 Shetland Mainland – North West**

Circular Walk G: HEYLOR

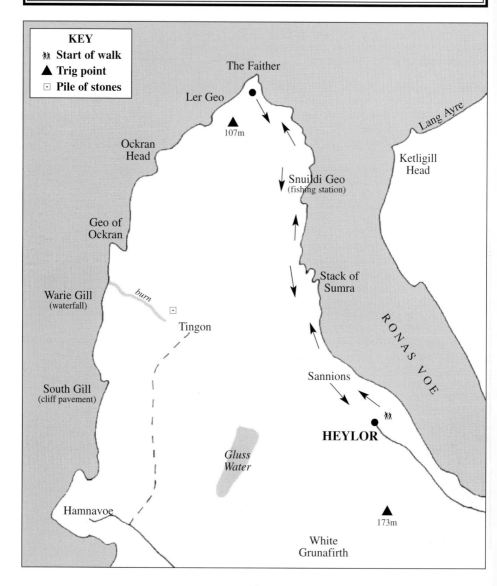

KEY
- 🏃 **Start of walk**
- ▲ **Trig point**
- ⊡ **Pile of stones**

The Faither

Ler Geo

Lang Ayre

▲ 107m

Ockran Head

Ketligill Head

Snuildi Geo
(fishing station)

Geo of Ockran

Warie Gill
(waterfall)

burn

⊡

Tingon

Stack of Sumra

R O N A S   V O E

South Gill
(cliff pavement)

Sannions

HEYLOR

Gluss Water

Hamnavoe

▲ 173m

White Grunafirth

A wonderful 'there and back' walk along the south shore of Ronas Voe to an outstanding area of impressive cliffs and on to The Faither with its caves and natural arches. For additional information see Walk 7.

This walk starts at Heylor where the unclassified road ends. This minor road starts at Urafirth where it heads north from the A970 past Assater. (Or alternatively, where it heads west from Swinister near Collafirth.)

On the way to Heylor visit the site of the Hollanders' Grave near the Pier at Skeo Head. Here Dutch sailors killed in action in 1674 are buried.

From Scorie Geo, with its natural arches the cliffs become ever more dramatic with attendant stacks off Weinnia to the four peaks of various heights which soar up from the base of the cliff at Sanda Calla. East of the ruined croft of Sannions is the Point of Quida Stack – a trunk of rock standing vertically out of the sea narrowing at its base. Above the red stacks of Burka Sumra is the ruined croft of Sumra. Cross a fence and descend Bratta Beck to view the waterfall at Geo Larradale. The burn from Helia Waters tumbles down some natural steps on its way to the sea.

Pass four stone ruins adjacent to a large reasonably flat area of rock – for drying fish? Go round Snuildi Geo and find three more ruined stone buildings, possibly former haaf fishing lodges, on a small promontory. Enjoy the view north of the land on the north side of Ronas Voe, particularly from Ketligill Head up to the point of Hevdadale Head.

Continue on to Galti Geo which offers the sight of the narrow, natural arch through Galti Stack and then make for the Faither Peninsula, with its small group of boulders and below it another natural arch.

The great thing is that here you turn round to return to Heylor the way you came and can enjoy this memorable walk again from a different approach.

Sanda Calla Stacks, Ronas Voe.

CIRCULAR WALK H ▆▆▆▆▆▆▆▆▆▆▆▆▆▆▆▆▆

COLLAFIRTH – RONAS HILL SUMMIT – COLLAFIRTH

6 miles (10 kms) : 3 hours

OS Maps: Explorer 469 Shetland Mainland – North West

A return walk from sea level to the top of Ronas Hill 1475ft (450m) Shetland's highest hill. Even in summer it can be pretty breezy on the summit and one needs to wrap up warm. Some of the finest views in Shetland and a prehistoric chambered cairn will be found on top, following a steady climb with nothing too taxing, if the wind be at all moderate. For further information about this walk see Walk 9.

From the junction at North Collafirth of the A970 and the road up Collafirth Hill climb

west. The road is not signposted. It will be found on the left just beyond the fir tree surrounded house called Forsà.

From the bottom of Collafirth Hill it takes about half an hour to reach some masts. Where the road ends at the second mast is a turning area and a red, granite cairn built by Scottish Natural Heritage. On it, under the heading 'A Walk to the Arctic', is an interpretive board highlighting the walk to Ronas Hill, the geology and the plant life of this very special

---

Circular Walk H: COLLAFIRTH – RONAS HILL SUMMIT – COLLAFIRTH

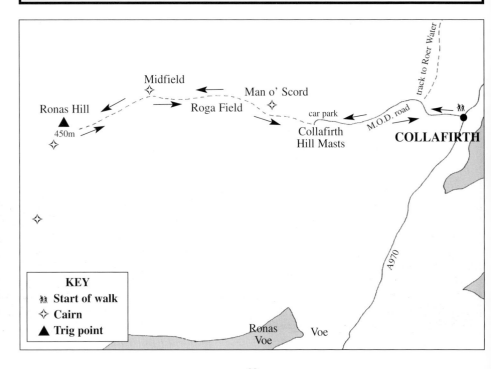

Trig point, Ronas Hill.

Chambered cairn, Ronas Hill.

Chambered cairn, Ronas Hill.

June. However, the weather may be awful and the hood of one's anorak useful to fend off the hailstones.

A few yards west some boulders have been set in a circle with a cross in it. To the south west is a well preserved chambered cairn which originally measured about 45ft in diameter. The single compartment chamber is reached through the entrance on the east and a passage about 5ft high. The chamber is built of massive blocks and is 4ft high, 5ft 6in long and 3ft broad. Many must have found sanctuary here over the centuries and your arrival may cause resting snow buntings, fieldfare or other sheltering birds to move on.

From the trig point return back down the route taken up Ronas Hill and Collafirth Hill to reach the start point at North Collafirth.

area. The Drongs are visible south west. A wheeled trackway heads north west to a loose stone cairn on Man O'Scord. Before reaching the cairn on Mid Field the 'heather line' will be reached and thereafter all is bare stone. The trig point on top of Ronas Hill should be visible. To avoid Grud Burn walk to the north of a small tarn and Shurgie Scord and pass another cairn before reaching the cairn protected trig point at the summit of Ronas Hill 1475ft (450m). Time taken from the bottom of Collafirth Hill will now be about one and a half hours. Even on a day of good weather the shelter provided by the trig point cairn can be very welcome. The views can be spectacular with a sweep of about 80 miles. Both the Muckle Flugga Lighthouse, north, and Fair Isle, south, can be visible – just the place to celebrate the longest day of the year in

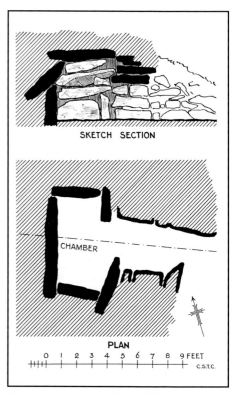

Chambered cairn plan, Ronas Hill.

CIRCULAR WALK I
COLLAFIRTH – RONAS HILL – LANG CLODIE WICK – ROER WATER – COLLAFIRTH

15 miles (20 kms) : 7 hours

OS Maps: Explorer 469 Shetland Mainland – North West

A long walk, full of interest, which keeps to the route of the Round Northmavine Trek as far as Lang Clodie Wick. The return to the A970 at the bottom of Collafirth Hill is made via Roer Water which has an interesting Neolithic homestead ruin. Adequate clothing and equipment is essential. Additional information about the route as far as Lang Clodie Wick is given in Walk 9.

Start by climbing Collafirth Hill, the road up which is on the left-hand side of the road shortly after passing the fir tree surrounded house of Forsà.

The road ends at some masts and a Scottish Natural Heritage cairn, from which proceed via Man O'Scord and Mid Field to the summit of Ronas Hill. Descend West to Ketligill Head and follow the coast north to Lang Clodie Wick. After taking a well earned rest here, and hopefully enjoying the magnificent waterfall, look for a Neolithic homestead site.

Cross the burn on stepping stones above the waterfall and climb the natural stone battlements to aim east from Lang Clodie Loch on the north side of the spirited burn flowing from Birka Water. Birka Water has its own

Ronas Hill summit.

93

waterfall on its south bank (water from Moshella Lochs) and little sandy beaches on its north banks. Then, it is a wander through peat banks and heather before reaching the waters of Clubbi Shuns and Roer Water. Keep to the northern side of these lochs which are distinguishable from each other by the little islets on them. Cross a wire fence with a wooden gate and about 80yds east (almost due

north from masts of Collafirth Hill) of the fence a 'homestead' is marked.

The Inventory describes the ruined building as an 'indeterminate structure', excavated in 1902 and 1904 but not sufficiently enough to reveal the original purpose of the building. It was entered from the south west, on the right side of which was a cell. On the left a narrow

Circular Walk I: COLLAFIRTH – RONAS HILL – LANG CLODIE WICK – ROER WATER – COLLAFIRTH

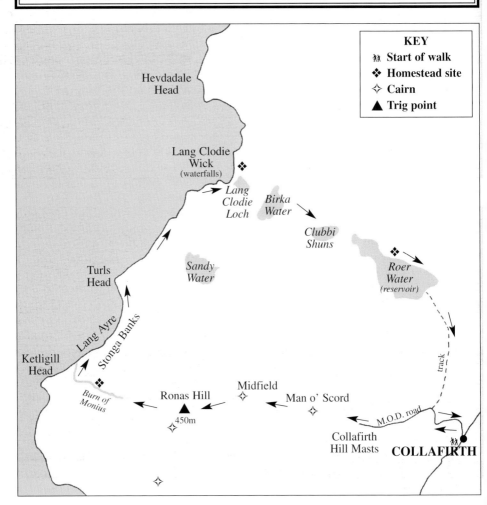

94

Lang Clodie Wick with waterfall on left.

Roer Water homestead.

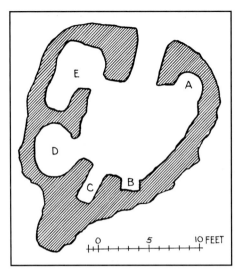

Roer Water homestead plan.

passage leads to a central chamber, circular in outline, with an internal diameter of 9ft 6ins. From this opened a number of recesses, three of rounded and two of rectangular form.

Roer Water is a reservoir and at its east end is a stone jetty, some stepping stones (just) and a little weir. One can now either follow the Burn of Roerwater down to The Brig or follow the service track – this is the easier option. Along the track are council concrete markers; above are cairns. When burn and track run closer together once more look across east to the steep ridge of rocks named the Beorgs of Housetter. 'Giant's Garden' is OS marked on the west slope. A visit to it involves fording the burn (take care here) and climbing up in the direction of a cairn. Before it is reached, in a boulder strewn area, the remains of a stone enclosure will be found. Here a giant of these parts stored cattle and other items acquired by plunder. To the east of Giant's Garden is a mass of angular stones; underneath some of the larger masses roomy and well sheltered cavities have been observed. It has been suggested that the cavities might have been utilised in former times as human habitation. Eventually the local people captured the Giant and threw him to his death from the top of the Beorgs. The Giant's Grave, today a ruined cairn and two standing stones, is situated on the W side of the A970 opposite the northerly half of the Loch of Housetter.

Return to the track, a coarse red scar resembling the surface of Mars, to rejoin the tarmac road up Collafirth Hill and descend to the A970 at North Colla Firth.

CIRCULAR WALK J

NORTH ROE – BEORGS OF UYEA NEOLITHIC AXE FACTORY – UYEA (ØYA) ISLE – NORTH ROE

10 miles (17 kms) : 5 hours (includes walking Uyea Isle)

OS Maps: Explorer 469 Shetland Mainland – North West

A walk on the wildside to reach the coast off which verdant Uyea (Øya) Isle lies. Check tide tables if aiming for access to Uyea Isle. The Neolithic axe factory is difficult to find but if you are successful you are asked not to remove anything from the site. Additional information may be found in Walk 10.

Drive to the village of North Roe. Pass the school on the left and the church on the right to commence the walk on the track, which goes all the way to Uyea Croft, on the north side of the CG station wooden building. Walk past

Greenfield and keep to the track which branches left of the Vatsendi Burn in a south west direction. The burn is one of the prettiest in Shetland, has a small weir but no sign of a mill ruin, though there is a ruined stone enclosure. One climbs into an area of peat banks before crossing a fence into a grazing area. Splash across a wide ford at the Burn of Sandvoe and at the next fence return to heather. Whimbrel may be spotted here. Pettadale Water is just to north whilst to the south the cairn on top of the Beorgs of Skelberry is visible.

Beorgs of Uyea cairn.

From the highest point of the track below Beorgs of Uyea the Ramna Stacks, Fethaland and Gloup Holm off north Yell can be seen. It will have taken about an hour to reach Mill Loch. One can stay on the track or leave it and climb up to the cairn above the south west shore. From this cairn walk north along the top of the hill to a second cairn. Super view from here includes Collafirth Hill masts.

Descend aiming north east towards a lower cairn. Half way down the hill, above the west end of the little loch connected north west to Mill Loch, is a boulder with a small cairn on it. This marks the site of a Neolithic axe factory and quarry.

A shelter made of granite blocks was made by prehistoric man by roofing the hollow where

Circular Walk J: NORTH ROE – BEORGS OF UYEA NEOLITHIC AXE FACTORY – UYEA (ØYA) ISLE – NORTH ROE

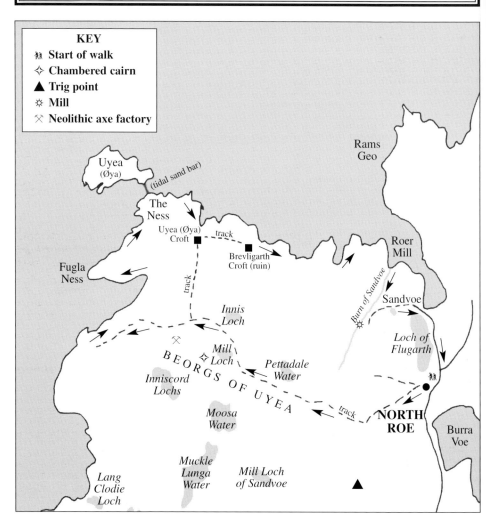

KEY
ᛃ Start of walk
✧ Chambered cairn
▲ Trig point
☼ Mill
✕ Neolithic axe factory

Neolithic axe factory, Beorgs of Uyea.

he had dug down beside a huge rock, about 12ft long. The rock has some))))) marks on it at the end near the opening to the cavity. The speckled or banded felsite rock quarried here only occurs in Britain in this area. The majority of Neolithic knives found in Shetland are fashioned from felsite and axes and maces made here were exported to Scotland and England. There are fragments of the felsite lying about which even in an unpolished state can be quite sharp today. Please help preserve Shetland's heritage by leaving any fragments where you may find them.

Walk north west to a 6ft high cairn built on top of a large red boulder and make your way west over various stone ruins to cross a single stone height wall, valley and wire fence to reach a wide track. Walk north and at the end of the track head north west to The Ness and Uyea Isle which can be accessed if the tide is well

out. It feels a bit spooky when first stepping out onto the sand between the mainland and the island. Follow the coastline east round North Wick and on to the ruined croft at Brevligarth at the end of the track. From Calder's Head to Sandvoe the coast walk can be quite taxing if very rewarding. A more direct route involves climbing inland up marshy The Hoga and Burra Too on the north slope of Saefti Hill. Descend to cross the Burn of Sandvoe which flows into the sea at Roer Mill.

It is worth a diversion to explore down the dale to the beach at Roer Mill, where there is a ruined booth (bod), although here was once the scene of an infamous incident. In 1774 a pirate ship anchored in Sand Voe and, following a dispute onboard, one of the pirates, Jacob Stays, was bound hand and foot and brought ashore. Here he was murdered by being buried

Uyea Isle.

alive, much to the horror of the islanders who were powerless to intervene.

Return up the burn to an excellently preserved ruin of a water mill where one crosses the burn to join the track which goes down past a small loch to the small, sheltered settlement at

Sandvoe. There is a sandy beach in front of the cemetery and those who have walked The Ness will cross a stile before reaching the fence at the road.

From Sandvoe walk the road south past the Loch of Flugarth to return to North Roe.

CIRCULAR WALK K

ISBISTER – FETHALAND – ISBISTER

6 miles (10 kms) : 3 hours

OS Maps: Explorer 469 Shetland Mainland – North West

A walk to the very tip of Mainland Shetland. Drive to where the road ends at Isbister. There is a private road which lies the other side of the gate and heads north.

No cars or dogs are allowed through this gate but there is a parking area and walkers are allowed access. This is a classic Shetland walk and not to be missed. Additional information can be found in Walk 11.

From the gate follow the track as it heads round Hill of Lanchestoo (trig point 130m) enjoying the view north of the Isle of

Fethaland. The isle is linked with Fethaland by a stony spit to the west of which huge boulders have been storm-tossed.

Here was once Shetland's busiest haaf fishing station. Today the ruins of over twenty fishing lodges stand silent round the shore. About 60 sixerns would have been stationed here between the beginning of June and the second week in August. The haaf fishing began in the early eighteenth century and was at its peak in 1809. The sixern, which was a boat with six oars and a square sail, fished up to forty miles from land mainly for cod and ling.

Fethaland.

101

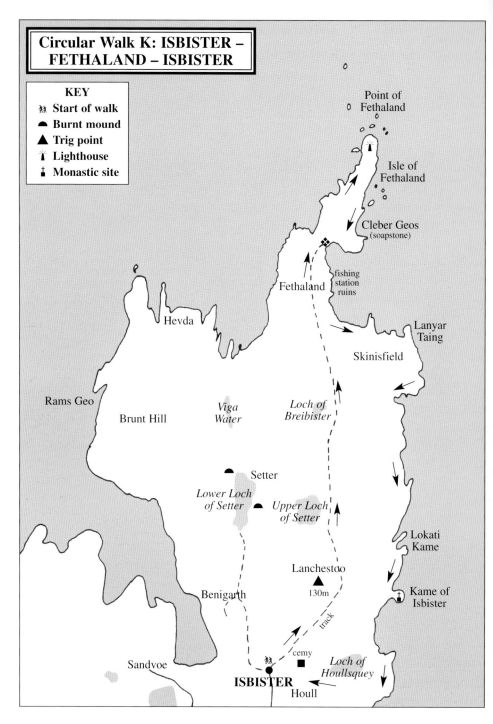

Circular Walk K: ISBISTER – FETHALAND – ISBISTER

KEY
- 👫 Start of walk
- 🔴 Burnt mound
- ▲ Trig point
- 🕯 Lighthouse
- ⚱ Monastic site

Point of Fethaland

Isle of Fethaland

Cleber Geos
(soapstone)

fishing station ruins

Fethaland

Hevda

Lanyar Taing

Skinisfield

Rams Geo

Viga Water

Loch of Breibister

Brunt Hill

Setter

Lower Loch of Setter

Upper Loch of Setter

Lokati Kame

Lanchestoo

130m

Kame of Isbister

Benigarth

Sandvoe

cemy

Loch of Houllsquey

ISBISTER

Houll

track

Fir Am gyaain ta da far haaf,
Becaase da wadder's fair,
An a boannie lok o fish we'll hae
Ta lay apo da ayre

'Gyaain ta da Far Haaf'
George Stewart

Fish landed at Uyea, which had no suitable beach, were also taken to Fethaland for drying. Dominating the approach by sea from the north west stands a 5ft cairn; above the shingle beach on the south east side of the isthmus are the remains of two well-constructed stone boat noosts. Behind the noosts on the green plateau, between them and the stone wall, are the remains of a 'homestead'. The Inventory originally listed this mound as a 'broch (probable)' but admitted that there were no traces of any surrounding defensive works. Today all that is visible is the arc of a semi-circular wall and it is classified as an Iron Age house site.

Ascend through the wall onto the 'isle' and keep to high ground near the precipitous west cliffs for sight of Burlee and most impressive Yellow Stack, near the lighthouse. Descend to the Point of Fethaland and after a three hour walk take a break and enjoy the view north over Stuack of the Ramna Stacks – once a bombing range and now an RSPB reserve. The northern extremity of the Point of Fethaland

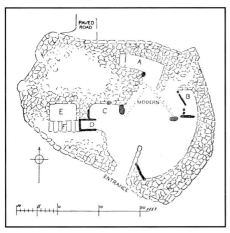

Fethaland homestead plan.

marks the harbour pilots' limit of the Port of Sullom Voe and tankers pick up and drop off pilots off this point.

Time now for us to turn south. The return along the east coast of the isle should include a study of a large rock face of steatite on the northern slope of Cleber Geo, where many generations of fishermen and others have carved names, hearts and dates. The oldest I have noticed is 1866. The Inventory notes that urns and bowls were cut out of the rock here, "the most extensive group of steatite workings in Shetland" and that, "exactly similar methods of working steatite were employed by the aborigines in many parts of North America".

Leave the Isle of Fethaland and head south east along the coast to Wick of Breibister and pass below the ruined croft of South House, the birthplace of photographer Jack Rattar (1876-1957) and the last inhabited house on Fethaland. Sadly Jack's father was drowned in the year of his birth but his Uncle Charles is remembered for being skipper of the last sixern, named the *Maggie*, to fish from Fethaland in the late 1890s. (see photograph page 55)

Jack Rattar (he changed his name from Ratter early in his professional career) became generally regarded as the best and best known of Shetland's early photographers. He was a pioneer of bird photography (and in 1926 a Shetland walrus). His pictures of Shetland landscapes can still "stir a longing in the hearts of the thousands of Shetlanders scattered all over the world, for in them love of their island home is intense".

Lanyar Taing protrudes north below the ruined croft and well preserved water mill of Skinisfield. Hibbert remarked that Fethaland is, "where grass is found to be so abundant and juicy that oxen feed theron both winter and summer", and there are many signs of ancient enclosures to be seen. The caves of Trumba attract sea birds, particularly kittiwakes. A large lump of quartz rock lies in the hill above the large sheep enclosure and very deep geo of Eislin Geo.

Climb up and over Ramna Beorgs and cross the plateau where Little Burn passes an ancient sheep cru. On Lokati Kame is an attractive natural arch below and the possible remains of a Celtic monastic site on top.

The building, rectilinear in structure, is similar to other known settlement ruins on the Kame of Isbister and Birrier, a site also to be viewed only from afar as access is now across a knife edge of rock.

Descend towards the valley leading to a beach below the Kame of Isbister. The Kame has been described by Dr K. O. Lamb as being the finest ancient coastal settlement site in the Northern Isles. The rock on which the settlement once stood is, "120ft high at the landward side and slopes 1 in 3 down towards the sea, giving a sloping grass-grown area, which is not visible from the land, of four-fifths of an acre. On the upper part of the slope are concentrated most of the 19 buildings now detectable". Twenty-three buildings were originally recorded here in the 1870s. Known locally as a 'Pictish graveyard', Dr Lamb considers this to be a monastic site possibly with Irish or Pict connections. Directly

opposite on the west coast of Yell at Birrier is another similar site. It is not worth even attempting to cross over the kame; a view can be obtained of the slope from top of Head of Virdibrig (OS Virdibreck) – a climb well worth the effort.

From here head west round the southern shore of Loch of Houllsquey to join a track which heads past a very overgrown water mill to reach Isbister an active crofting area and place of ancient settlement. There is no evidence of a broch here but there is a ruin of a burnt mound by the burn before one reaches Houll, the site of a medieval chapel dedicated to St. Magnus and the cemetery.

Here are to be seen three memorials made of wood and also a memorial to a certain Captain William Tulloch of Puddles who died 20th March, 1915 aged 89:

'We saw him fading like a star
But could not make him stay
We tended him with greatest care
Till God took him away'.

What a good innings: what care to the end!

Pund, by J. D. Rattar.

CIRCULAR WALK L ▄▄▄▄▄▄▄▄▄▄

THE GIANT'S TRAIL

5 miles (8 kms) : 3 hours

OS Maps: Explorer 469 Shetland Mainland – North West

A fun walk exploring the area of Northmavine where the legend of a giant lives on in the names of various features round Colla Firth. The route takes one from Lochend – The Brig Collafirth (Giant's Basket) – Burn of Roerwater (Giant's Garden) – Beorgs of Housetter (Giant's Fall) – Loch of Housetter (Giant's Grave).

"… and there were giants in those days." In Unst the names of the giants Saxa and Herman live on but their Colla Firth cousin has lost his. Let us therefore call him Raun (Old Norse for stone-heap; stony ground, from which the name Ronis (Ronas) Hill derived), because his activities are all stone and ridge of hills related.

Raun was 19ft tall and must have looked awesome; he was a rustler and is quite likely to have had his main dwelling where the mansion of Lochend stands today; it is such a splendid site. So start the walk here and cross the Ayre to follow the coastline to The Brig. Above the road the Inventory reports there were two cairns about 30yds from the road which appear to have been from 36ft to 42ft in diameter.

The Brig – Giant's Maeshie.

Folklore relates that Raun sought to extend the territorial range of his criminal activities by linking Collafirth to Yell by a causeway across Yell Sound. Unfortunately, the nets holding the stones which he carried down to the sea shore were not strong enough and all the rocks fell out just before he got there. Subsequently the boulder strewn area was known as the 'Giant's

Basket' or 'Maeshie' (a maeshie was a net constructed for carrying hay or corn).

Walk up the Burn of Roer Water and when below the cairn on the Beorgs climb up east into a boulder strewn area where, half way up the slope of the hill, the remains of a stone enclosure will be found. Here Raun stored

Circular Walk L: THE GIANT'S TRAIL

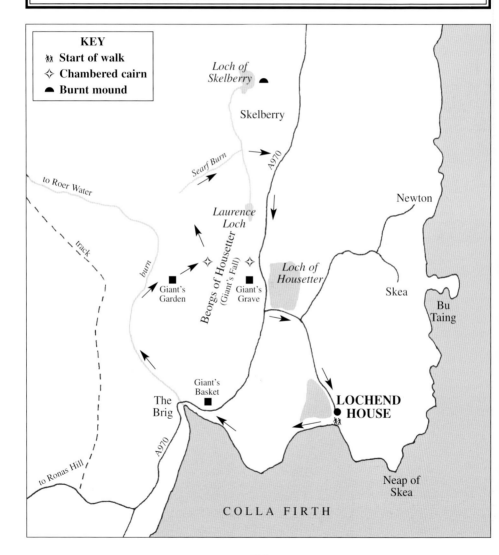

KEY
🏃 Start of walk
✧ Chambered cairn
▲ Burnt mound

Loch of Skelberry

Skelberry

Searf Burn

A970

to Roer Water

Newton

Laurence Loch

Beorgs of Housetter
(Giant's Fall)

track

burn

Giant's Garden

Giant's Grave

Loch of Housetter

Skea

Bu Taing

Giant's Basket

The Brig

A970

LOCHEND HOUSE

to Ronas Hill

Neap of Skea

COLLA FIRTH

Giant's Garden.

cattle and other items acquired by plunder. It has been suggested that to the east of the enclosure, in a mass of angular stones, were well sheltered cavities where people could have been accommodated. There is one description of several chambers being connected by narrow passageways. However, today no sign of artificial construction can be seen.

But Raun could not reign forever. Eventually the local people rose up, attacked and captured him in his lair and carried him off to the escarpment on the east side of Beorgs of Housetter, which can be viewed from the cairn, and flung him to his doom (Giant's Fall).

Descend to the A970 road just north of Laurence Loch via Searf Burn and walk south to discover where he landed and was buried. On the west side of the road, on flat ground opposite the north end of Loch of Housetter, is a heap of stones which is all that remains of a heel-shaped cairn once 27ft in diameter. It is

possible to see the internal chamber by clambering over the rubble. Once known as the 'Trowie Knowe' or Fairy Knoll it is made up of large red stones which, the Inventory says, suffered seriously from being used as a quarry when the public road was built. But we know better. Its perfect form was undoubtedly shattered when Raun landed on top of it when catapulted down from the Beorgs above! Two hundred yards south of this cairn two standing stones with a cairn will be found. No features of the cairn are visible but the stones, named 'Giant's Grave', are prominent despite the backdrop of the high and very rugged scree. The stones are set roughly due north and south and are rough undressed blocks of red granitic rock. The south stone is larger, rising 8ft with a girth of 10ft 6ins. Under it, tradition tells, lies the head of the Giant Raun. The north stone is separated from it by a distance of 19ft. It stands 6ft 6ins. Under this stone lie Raun's feet.

Dismayed by the loss of one chambered cairn the builders built another one nearby. It is

107

reported to have been built (not yet identified by me) on a steeply sloping shelf on the rocky east side of the Beorgs, above and slightly west south west of Trowie Knowe (so beware of them too). Small and well preserved from falling giants it measures 16ft 9ins across the straight facade on the south east side, and 17ft 2ins from the facade to the rear of the cairn.

The chamber is exposed, the walling being visible to a height of 3ft and is entered by a passage opening from the front of the facade.

The Giant's Trail is completed by leaving his grave and walking south to follow the road left below the Loch of Housetter and so back to Lochend.

Giant's grave.

CIRCULAR WALK M ▮▮▮▮▮▮▮▮▮▮

OLLABERRY – QUEYFIRTH – OLLABERRY

5 miles (8 kms) : 3 hours

OS Maps: Explorer 469 Shetland Mainland – North West

Ollaberry, one of the "prettiest spots in Shetland", (Dr. Cowie) is the start/finish of this enjoyable walk. Additional information will be found in Walk 12.

Commence this walk in the spacious car park of Ollaberry church, the burial ground of which contains some fine decorated tombstones. Walk through the village passing the Haa and follow the road below the outcrop, The Berg, to the junction right to Leon. Climb the steep hill and admire the view either from the road or the trig point on Hill of Ollaberry (118m). It was at the top of the hill to Leon that

Ollaberry kirk and manse, by John Reid (1869).

I came across a Japanese hawkfinch, which caused quite a flap at the time. It was the first one to be seen in Shetland and there was a great deal of speculation on how far the oriental bird had travelled. Four weeks later it flew into Burravoe, Yell, and took up residence near The Old Manse!

Descend to the footbridge at the head of Loch of Queyfirth. Proceed up Quey Firth and descend to explore the ayre behind which is a splendid tidal basin, the Loch of Queyfirth, which never ebbs out. There are some stone ruins on the ayre and at the south end possibly a ruined, stone otter trap. Decide whether you

are going to sensibly walk round the loch to a footbridge or, if the tide is out, splash through low water and climb onto the lower slopes of Hill of Ollaberry. At Hogan is a very large ruin of what must have been a magnificent croft house and associated gardens and buildings. At Norwick is another croft ruin which looks down on to the beach. A large stone dyke, today backed by a modern fence with a metal gate, marks the frontier line to the hill area named Back of Ollaberry. Here a shallow depression, which crosses the end of the rounded headland from east to west, is the line of a geological fault. The depression can be followed down to the beach where it is

Circular Walk M: OLLABERRY – QUEYFIRTH – OLLABERRY

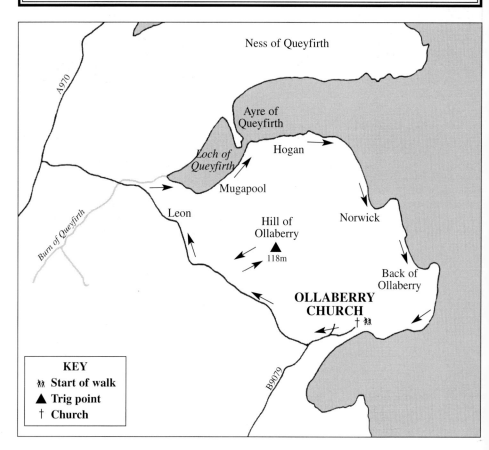

110

The Japanese Hawkfinch.

exposed as dark, hard rock. A walk over the headland provides a superb route to end this walk. Climb up to the cliff line above Saberstone. At the hill's peak 62m (186ft) there is no mark but just below, on the west slope, is a small rectangular concrete slab. Descend, passing Pigeon Cove and Otter Had, where there are the remains of an old sheep pund, and enter the Bay of Ollaberry. The walled burial ground brings this walk to a grave conclusion; go to its right and follow the wall to a gate over which is the parking area at the west end of the church, which, fittingly for a township once named Olafsberg, is dedicated to St. Olaf.

Dr Cowie thought Ollaberry, "one of the prettiest spots in Shetland. On a fine summer evening nothing in the far north can excel the beauty of the scene".

CIRCULAR WALK N

NORTH GLUSS – YAMNA FIELD – MILL KNOWES – BURRALAND – SOUTH GLUSS

5 miles (8 kms) : 3 hours

OS Maps: Explorer 469 Shetland Mainland – North West

Circular Walk N: NORTH GLUSS – YAMNA FIELD – MILL KNOWES – BURRALAND – SOUTH GLUSS

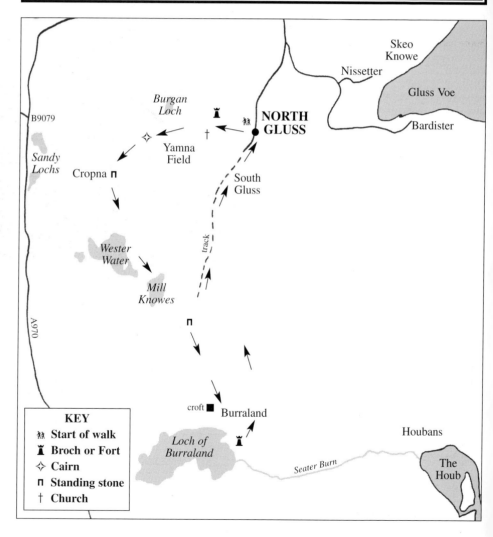

KEY

⚔ Start of walk
♜ Broch or Fort
✧ Cairn
� Standing stone
† Church

Medieval chapel site, prehistoric bolt hole, two broch sites and standing stones – all have been recorded near Gluss. To reach Gluss you will have passed Eela Water which Tudor says should be, "properly speaking Ola's Water". At Nissetter is Ola's Broch (Skeo Knowe on OS) and a souterrain was discovered nearby in 1900 but it has now disappeared.

To cover the inland sites the following route is suggested:

From North Gluss climb up the hill east to reach the escarpment above at Burgan. There are twin peaks and the southerly rocky hillock, 300ft above sea level, is the site of a broch. There is not much evidence of it today but one can still enjoy a commanding view of the countryside around. In the National Museum are two oval polished knives of dark porphyritic stone found here. A small rough stone enclosure stands in the hollow of the ruin. On the flat area to the north of the hillock are the outlines of two turf/stone enclosures.

The medieval chapel site and burial ground can be found by following the wire fence down from the south east corner of the broch mound for about 100ft to a flat area cut into the hill. The chapel has been reduced by stone removal, though some large stones remain, and no details of its size and plan survive, except that it was orientated east to west. The graveyard, terraced into the hillside, is enclosed by a turf-covered wall of large stones. No graves can be seen.

I was informed that, if one leaps up and down some areas sound hollow underfoot. Not wishing to risk a disappearing act I have not undertaken that method of archaeological exploration.

Return to the broch and descend west to pass through red granite dry stone wall by a derelict croft to the south of Burgan Loch. Cross Yamna Field and climb to the small cairn on the summit west. Superb views here. On a tongue of land forming a shoulder of the hill 50ft below is a magnificent standing stone, in the shape of a massive 10ft high red granite

Cropna – washes its feet in Sandy Lochs on Yule morning.

boulder, which surveys the junction of the Hillswick and Ollaberry roads through the twin waters of Sandy Lochs.

This stone is known as Cropna and according to folklore it descends the hill on Yule morning to wash its feet in the waters of Sandy Lochs. Further to the north an even bigger boulder, Bonna, is fortunately not so mobile. Return to the cairn and proceed south for Wester Water. This loch has many features and is connected to the smaller loch below Mill Knowes perhaps should be named Mill Loch; a substantial ruin of a water mill stands beside the burn connecting the two waters. Walk the east shore of the loch past a stone ruin and on

Wester Water standing stone.

the southern slope of Mill Knowes, just before a final descent to a track, is the standing stone of Wester Water. One suggestion is that it once formed part of a greatly ruined field wall of indeterminate age. It is a rough undressed boulder of granite rock 3ft 6ins high and a girth at base of 7ft 6ins. The inventory states, "there is nothing to suggest that it is an ancient monument".

It makes little impact standing next to it but viewed from some distance south is quite prominent. One hundred and fifty yards west is a ruined water mill above which the trig point (121m) on Ness Vird is visible. Walk south to Loch of Burraland, keeping out of grazing land round the croft by following the outside of a wire fence to the shore. On a little point projecting from the north east shore of the loch is a grassy mound which rises about 20ft above the water surmounted by a small circular stone building – a former lime kiln. There is a stone ruin on the north side of the mound but of the Burraland Broch construction itself, there is little sign; the odd stone around the base of the mound may indicate the outer wall face. "One of the few

Burraland Broch.

brochs in Shetland that are at a distance from the sea". (Russell)

Return to the track below Mill Knowes and walk back to Gluss and maybe take suitable refreshment, because Gluss is celebrated in song as a place where drinking can cause a certain hesitancy in speech.

'I come fae Yell, come fae Yell, come fae Yell'
'I come fae Northmavine'
'I come fae Gluss'
's-s-s-s-s so do I'.

'I Come Fae Yell'
Helly Hoy Review
Harry Kay

CIRCULAR WALK O ████████████

BRAEWICK – THE RUNK – HEADS OF GROCKEN – GILLIE BURN (SAND WICK)

5 miles (8 kms) : 3 hours

OS Maps: Explorer 469 Shetland Mainland – North West

I can vividly recall the first time I walked this magnificent stretch of cliff scenery. The weather was perfect and the sun blazed down on to the Heads of Grocken and The Runk, making an indelible impression. One can walk either 'there and back' along the cliffs or opt to return along the B9078 road. If possible, allow time (half an hour) to visit the burnt mound of Burnside. For further information see Walk 5.

Start the walk at the junction of the B9078 Hillswick-Stenness road at the junction to

Braewick. Walk down the road to the houses and go left of the last house to walk down to Braewick Loch – a loch which twice in 100 years has drained away. Cross the shingle beach and start to climb up, below Clave, to reach a stile and view four stacks close inshore, two of which appear to be on kissing terms when viewed from The Neap. On the shoulder of the cliff, beware an evil deep cleft, 22yds long, in from the cliff edge. It is a veritable Joseph's pit; sheep bones at bottom indicate how dangerous it is.

Circular Walk O: THE HEADS OF GROCKEN

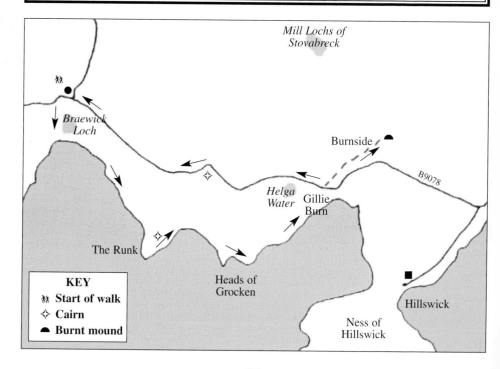

116

A cairn on the rising ground is a good vantage point to admire the stubby twin peaks of The Runk. Inland another cairn on Watch Hill may attract interest. It is some 18ft in diameter, marked by a kerb of stones which are placed round the circumference.

The Heads of Grocken is a dramatic bluff of which there are many stacks and further out to sea, The Drongs. From Grocken look down on Hillswick where the notable restored old manse and Hillswick Ness are clearly visible. Descend past a ruined, red granite stone croft ruin to follow the cliffs to the road passing above Grey Face, a dark headland. The walk ends at the deep ravine of Gillie Burn which is only slightly more alarming than a cattle grid leading to the road. Decision time. One can walk either back the route taken to get here in about two hours or walk back along the road in 45 minutes. A ten minute walk south along the road brings one to Burnside Croft and its remarkable burnt mound. On the left of the road, cross a gate and walk to the twin mounds by bearing slightly left into the slope of the hill. Somehow, a complete stone trough made of granite and sandstone has survived. Two other slabs lie on each side of the trough. So, if you decide to visit this burnt mound and return to Braewick along the road allow one hour fifteen minutes from the time Gillie Burn was reached.

Northmavine water mill.

FOOTNOTE

This completes the walking guide to Northmavine. If you have accomplished all 120 miles of the Round Northmavine Trek during the period of a single holiday in Northmavine then you are to be particularly congratulated. Long distance walker or Sunday stroller, all will have enjoyed some aspect of Northmavine, and, as you cross Mavis Grind heading south, there is time to share a salute given by Dr Cowie when he quoted the poet Claud Halcro on his departure:

"Farewell to Northmavine,
Grey Hillswick, farewell –
To the calms of thy haven,
To the storms on thy fell."

Northmavine contains all that is best in Shetland and it is well worth preserving. In the words of Dr Tom Anderson to the young people of these islands. "Your heritage is your treasure house – keep it going."

NOTES

Geology – The north coast of Northmavine boasts the oldest rocks in Shetland. In Eshaness are basalt lava cliffs and the black igneous rocks are studded with agate and occasionally amethyst. Near Hillswick kyanite, garnet, serpentine and actinolite may be found.

Plants – 15 arctic flowering plants are to be found on Ronas Hill including alpine lady's-mantle, trailing azalea and moss campion.

Birds – Divers, skuas, dunlin and merlin breed in the area. The nearest RSPB reserve to Northmavine is on Ramna Stacks and therefore only approachable by boat. Here the guillemots, razorbills, puffins and kittiwakes can be spotted. Fulmar, herring and great black backed gulls may be seen all round the coast.

Mammals – Otters are shy but may be seen, particularly on Hillswick Ness and in Sullom Voe. Common and grey seals are usually in evidence. Sheep are everywhere and Shetland ponies in small numbers also feature in the Northmavine landscape.

Shops – There are two shops in Northmavine: Hillswick and the Ollaberry Co-operative.

ACKNOWLEDGEMENTS

I am indebted to the authors and editors of the following books, songs, magazine articles and people who have helped me:

The Enigma of "Johnnie Notions" Williamson	Dr I. D. Conacher	2001
Journal of Medical Biography		
Shetland	Jill Slee Blackadder	2003
Songs and Sights of Shetland	Christine M. Guy	1995
To Introduce the Orkneys and Shetlands	Iain F. Anderson	1939
Northwards by Sea	Gordon Donaldson	1978
Shetland Archaeology	Edited Brian Smith	1985
Hay & Company	James R. Nicolson	1982
Place Names of Shetland	Jakob Jakobson	1936
Shetland Dictionary	John Graham	1979
The Medieval Churches and Chapels of Shetland	R. G. Cant	1975
A guide to Prehistoric Shetland	Noel Fojut	1981
A guide to Shetland's Breeding Birds	Bobby Tulloch	1992
A Description of the Shetland Islands	Samuel Hibbert	1822
Shetland	Robert Cowie	1874
Guide to Shetland	T. M. Y. Manson	1942
The Orkneys and Shetland	John R. Tudor	1883
Shetland III ('The Inventory')	Royal Commission on the Ancient and Historic Monuments of Scotland	1946
Reminiscences of a Voyage to Shetland	Christian Ployen	1896
A Brief Description of Orkney, Zetland etc.	John Brand	1701
Description of Zetland Islands	Thomas Gifford	1733
Shetland Life Magazine	Ed. James R. Nicolson	
Shetland Field Studies Walks	Jill Slee Blackadder	1992
Orkney and Shetland	George Low	1774
Art Rambles in Shetland	John Reid	1869
Cloud Cover	Derek Gilpin Barnes	1943
Offshore – A North Sea Journey	Al Alvarez	1986
Proceedings of the Society of Antiquaries of Scotland		1951-52
1. Chambered cairn and working gallery, Beorgs of Uyea	Laurence Scott and Charles Calder	
2. Partial excavation of a broch at Sae Breck	Charles Calder	
3. Unexcavated Stone Age house – sites	Isleburgh 1 to 4	
'I Come Fae Yell' Helly Hoy Review	Harry Kay	1952
The Chambered Tombs of Scotland	Audrey Shore Henshall	1965
The Windswept Isles	Elizabeth Balneaves	1977
Coastal Settlements of the North (Scottish Archaeological Forum Volume 5.)	Raymond Lamb	1973
The Northern Isles	Alexander Fenton	1978
Burnt Mound Papers	R. John Cruse	
Shetland Folk Book Vol. 3 – The Islesburgh Eagle	L. G. Scott	1957
The 'Diana' of Hull	Arthur Credland	1979
Shetland & Orkney Journal	Samuel Dunn	1822 – 1825
(edited Harold Bowes)		1976
Ringing Strings	Tom Anderson	1983

ACKNOWLEDGEMENTS

Books:

Scottish Pictures	Samuel Green	1891
Pictures from Shetland's Past	Fred Irvine	1955
Sons and Daughters of Shetland 1800-1900	Margaret Stuart Robertson	1991

The Royal Commission on the Ancient and Historic Monuments of Scotland for the drawings of Broch (probable) Fethaland, March Cairn, Roer Water Homestead, Ronas Hill Chambered Cairn, Hamnavoe Broch, Punds Water Chambered Cairn, Gateside Chambered Cairn – © Royal Commission on the Ancient and Historic Monuments of Scotland.

Scots Magazine 'J. D. Rattar'	A. T. Cluness	March 1957

Songs:

'Gyaain ta da Far Haaf'	George Stewart
(Set to music by Tom Anderson)	
'Ronas Voe'	Frank Chadwick (1920-2006)

(Set to music by Ronald Cooper: © held by Shetland Music. Both are published in the book, *Songs and Sights of Shetland*, compiled by Christine M. Guy: Published by Shetland Arts Trust in association with the Education Department of Shetland Islands Council ©1995 Shetland Arts Trust).

Otter at Nibon photograph; Edward Thomas. The Natural Museums of Scotland : photographs of bronze horse figurine and the Gunnister Man – © The National Museums of Scotland. J. D. Rattar photographs of Charles Ratter and Punds – © The Shetland Museum. Photograph of Tom Anderson and Shetland's Young Heritage 1983 – Dennis Coutts. Cross near Stenness and Uyea Isle sand bar © Christine M. Guy. All other photographs were taken by the author.

The Shetland Museum and the Shetland Library for the help and unfailing courtesy of all staff. John Williamson, North Roe. Margaret Roberts, Gluss. Drew and Elizabeth Cromarty, Loch End. Jim Mainland, Nibon. Terry Mayes, RAF Sullom Voe researcher. Val Turner, County Archaeologist for advice on ancient sites. Dr Mortimer Manson for his recollections of Northmavine men. Bill Manson, Mangaster. Gary Worral, Islesburgh House. Margaret Stuart Robertson, Shetland researcher. Theo and Betty Fullerton. "Maggie's Kettle" cartoon by Bill Jardine.

I am also particularly grateful to: Catherine Ginger who prepared this book for publication. Louis Johnson, formerly Head Teacher of North Roe School, who kindly read through my original draft in meticulous detail.

I am also grateful for the support and encouragement of the Northmavine Initiative at the Edge group (IatE) and the Hillswick and Eshaness Regeneration Development group (HEARD).

All publications in this series owe their existence to the 'Around the Isles' articles by 'Hundiclock' published in *Sullom Voe Scene*.

TANGWICK HAA

Details of opening times can be obtained by telephoning Tangwick Haa – (01806) 503389 or Visit Shetland – (01595) 693434.

Details of accommodation in Northmavine and Shetland, generally, are published each year by Visit Shetland, Market Cross, Lerwick. Telephone Lerwick (01595) 693434.